Social Forms

David Zwirner Books

Social Forms A Short History of Political Art Christian Viveros-Fauné

I.

Each dream finds at last its form; there is a drink for every thirst, and
love for every heart. And there is no better way to spend your life than
in the unceasing preoccupation of an idea—of an ideal.
—Gustave Flaubert, 1857

Some convictions take root early.

When I was nine years old, I turned the radio on and heard the signal
jump from George Harrison's "My Sweet Lord" to Eusebio Lillo and
Ramón Carnicer's "Canción nacional," Chile's national anthem. Like
every other station on the dial, the one I tuned into on September 11, 1973,
followed that patriotic number with a full day of marching songs from the
army, navy, air force, and national police. Even as a boy, I knew that back-
to-back military hymns could only mean one thing—the streets and the
airwaves had been invaded by the so-called forces of order.

Three years later, when I was twelve, my father, my mother, my sister,
my brother, and I drove a dozen miles from our then home in Greenbelt,
Maryland, to The Phillips Collection in Washington, DC, to look at
art. What that meant eluded me, until I came upon something unusual.
Crammed inside a thirteen-by-twenty-four-foot room were four large
paintings by the New York artist Mark Rothko. I remember watching them
vibrate—green, tangerine, red, and ocher presences—and connecting
them, bizarrely, to my enduring impressions of Chile's coup d'etat.
Energized by Rothko's fearsome dramas, these paintings jumped the track
of normal life and lodged themselves deep in my memory.

Twelve years hence, a third experience reconciled me to the idea that the
two things that had most shaped my life—politics and the visual art I'd fallen
madly in love with—might be intimately related. Seeing a dozen wartime prints
by Francisco de Goya y Lucientes at Madrid's Museo del Prado convinced me,
both rationally and emotionally, that there is no greater work of art than that
which critically engages one's own time. If the union of art and politics delivers
masterpieces only infrequently, years of close looking have taught me why this
might be so—arguably, political art is the hardest art to do well.

"I always wanted my works—whatever happened in the studio—
to look more like what was going on outside the window," Robert
Rauschenberg told an interviewer in 1964, the year after he memorialized
the murdered John F. Kennedy in his silk-screen portrait *Retroactive I*.
A century and a half earlier, Goya had addressed the obligations of the late
eighteenth-century imagination with similar forthrightness. "The sleep of
reason produces monsters," he wrote beneath his etching of a man assailed
by goggle-eyed, power-hungry creatures. "Imagination deserted by reason
creates impossible, useless thoughts. United with reason, imagination is
the mother of all art and the source of all its beauty."

Somewhere between those two statements thrive two fundamental
ambitions for modern and contemporary art that initially found their footing
among the barricades and battlefields of post-Enlightenment Europe. The
first of these goals proposes that art may—at times explicitly and at others
obliquely—act as a witness to history (this ultimately privileges storytelling
over formal considerations or art for art's sake). Concomitantly, art that
witnesses history finds itself uniquely positioned to oppose illiberalisms of
both the left and the right; it may critique, goad, provoke, condemn, and
generally engage political power directly without ever having to resort to
methods such as censorship, political coercion, or violence.

Like Europe during the first decade of the nineteenth century and the
US in the 1960s, our time has seen its share of unrest and calamity. Where
the Peninsular War (1808–14) resulted in vast destruction and millions of
deaths, Syria's civil war (2011–present) has cost five hundred thousand
lives and triggered one of the largest refugee crises in human history—of
the sixty-eight million people currently displaced around the world, twelve
million have been forced from their homes in Syria. Where the murders of
JFK and Medgar Evers in 1963, Malcolm X in 1965, and Martin Luther
King Jr. and Robert F. Kennedy in 1968 plunged the US into a spiral of
violence and political instability, a plague of police murders of unarmed
black citizens and a pandemic of school shootings have blown AR-15-sized
bullet holes in America's social fabric.

The societies of the United States and Europe—the steady centers
of postwar order for more than seventy years—now find themselves
disoriented, divided, and destabilized by a global plot that seeks to reverse
the course of world history and replace representative liberal democracies
with ideologically indeterminate populist nationalisms. Where countries
such as Chile, Argentina, and South Africa once suffered under the boot
of brazen autocrats, the US, the United Kingdom, and newer European
democracies such as Poland, Hungary, and Romania have fallen under the
sway of jingoistic isolationist policies, authoritarian politicians, or both.
The West took a sharp turn off the road to internationalism and improved
representative democracy in 2017. The world slalomed from order to

disorder, from globalism to protectionism, from contained instability to capricious brinksmanship. In the US, the presidency of Barack Obama gave way to that of Donald Trump.

If it is the artist's job to be a witness to his time in history, it stands to reason that it should be the critic's job to transcribe important instances of that testimony in the history books. In furtherance of this idea, I'd like to to cite George Orwell's mission as a writer. "What I have most wanted to do is to make political writing into an art," he declared in his 1946 essay "Why I Write." Since I began writing about art twenty-three years ago, my ambition has been exactly the opposite: to make writing about art political. This book is a modest attempt to advance that goal.

II.

The present is only faced, in any generation, by the artist . . . The absolute indispensability of the artist is that he alone, in the encounter with the present, can give the pattern of recognition. He alone has the sensory awareness to tell us what our world is made of. He is more important than the scientist.
—Marshall McLuhan, 1968

This volume provides a short, highly personal, nonexhaustive reckoning of art's engagement with power from 1810 to the present through fifty short essays on as many examples of epoch-defining political art.

From Goya's *The Disasters of War* (1810–20) to Picasso's nightmarish 1937 panorama *Guernica* to The Silence=Death Project's poster *SILENCE= DEATH* (1987), which came to define the AIDS activist movement in the 1980s and 1990s, this book aims to trace a line across multiple eras and geographies to chronicle the willful, unruly, yet inspiring history of political art. That history has affected millions. In our time, it has become progressively more charged as artists—and their increasingly global audience—react to momentous contemporary events such as the global migration crisis, climate change, Brexit, and the election of Donald Trump.

Arranged chronologically as connected accounts of representative artworks, each of the book's fifty essays relays how some of the world's greatest artists have dealt with political crises over the past two hundred years. These are snapshots of artists as they stare down, reflect on, and decry violent revolutions, modern warfare, enduring poverty, the multigenerational crime of racism, systematic sexual discrimination, the rise of consumer culture, and the challenges of technology, among other catastrophes.

Is political art protest art? Is it propaganda? Is it activism? Is all art political? This book takes on emblematic artworks that tackle these questions while it underscores the importance of these contributions to the art of the future. Though the book focuses primarily on the history of Western art, it also highlights fundamental contributions made by artists from other regions, including Latin America, Asia, and the Middle East.

This volume looks to create a group portrait of political art for the internet age—a time when artists find themselves responding to world events by negotiating between conventionally Kantian aesthetic objects and open-ended social processes. If certain contemporary artworks have augmented their handmade "aura" in the age of the World Wide Web (along with their financial value), other immaterial, process-based examples of what is called "socially engaged art" have grown in stature, becoming some of the most important works of our era.

The driving idea behind these essays is not only to consider political art in all its guises but also to establish a useful historical record where few others exist. As Orwell said in "Why I Write," the opinion that art should have nothing to do with politics is itself political. Conversely, this makes all art political, either on purpose or by omission—doubly so at times of social upheaval. In those heightened and dangerous circumstances, to quote James Baldwin, another great political artist, the challenge is in the moment, and the time is always now.

Francisco de Goya y Lucientes

The Disasters of War (1810–20, published 1863)

Grande hazaña. con muertos.

Francisco de Goya y Lucientes (1746–1828) is where this book about art and politics begins. Years after his death, he remains the hinge upon which modern art turns. After starting out as a provincial artist, he became Spain's most popular court painter and the most important commentator of his era. Often referred to as the last of the old masters and the first of the moderns, Goya was also the first great political artist of modern times.

For sheer force of sustained vision, no single piece of antiwar art matches the originality and ferocity of *The Disasters of War*, a series of eighty aquatints, complete with caustic captions, made by the Spanish artist Francisco de Goya. Perpetrated as a response to the spectacular butchery of the Peninsular War, the world's first guerrilla conflict, these searing images have burrowed into the world's collective memory with the lasting shock of war photographs and the internet's rawest videos.

Broadly speaking, Goya's images fall into three groups. Forty-six plates describe episodes of war and great cruelty committed by Napoleon's soldiers against the Spanish pueblos and vice versa. The second, a group of eighteen prints, takes as its subject the great famine that devastated Goya's own city of Madrid between 1811 and 1812. The third, which he titled *Caprichos enfáticos*, or "emphatic caprices"—with a view to invoking *Los caprichos* (1796–98), his previous suite of satirical etchings—allegorically documents what critic and Goya scholar Robert Hughes once called "the disasters of peace." Among these were the return of royal absolutism to Spain, the abolishing of the country's liberal 1812 constitution, and the restoration of Christianity's early modern precursor to Taliban terror: the Spanish Inquisition.

Long before the development of the photographic camera, Goya provided visual reportage from Europe's most dangerous conflict zone. If he didn't actually witness many of the horrors of war that he depicted, his drawings provided a fundamental kind of wartime testimonial. Today, even his most fantastical depictions seem to labor, morally if not altogether factually, in the service of truth.

One such event, seen to the left, is depicted in plate 39 of the *Disasters*. A sickening array of human body parts hang from a tree like Christmas lights—a headless and armless torso, a bodiless head, two arms tied together, and a castrated corpse. Goya describes the kind of mutilation that advertises, then as now, brutality as a fearsome worldview. Its caption reads blackly: *Grande hazaña! Con muertos!* or "Great feat! With dead men!"

This bleak image forecasts the millions upon millions of lives that would be sacrificed at the altar of systematic violence in the centuries to come—from Waterloo to the Nazi death camps to ISIS's mass beheadings. In John Milton's oxymoronic formulation, what Goya depicted in this and other *Disasters* was hell itself: "No light, but rather darkness visible."

Eugène Delacroix

July 28: Liberty Leading the People
(1830)

Eugène Delacroix (1798–1863) was the leading romantic painter in France. Depicting dramatic scenes from contemporary history and literature, he emphasized emotional content over rationality. His greatest artwork has been cribbed by, among others, a wildly popular Broadway production and the British rock band Coldplay.

Behold the image of revolution made heroic.

This painting, which hangs in the Louvre, in Paris, represents a pivotal moment in French history—when violent protests led to the abdication of an unpopular king and his replacement by a more liberal ruler. It is a filter through which many subsequent images of revolution may be interpreted, from Sergei Eisenstein's footage of the Bolsheviks storming the Winter Palace (restaged in 1920, three years after the event) to UPI photographs of Fidel Castro's *barbudos* entering a liberated Havana to iPhone pictures of the Libyan uprising during the Arab Spring.

Like Francisco de Goya's *The Disasters of War* (1810–20), *Liberty Leading the People* eschews narratives of the Greek and Roman past for the heat of contemporary events. Eugène Delacroix's masterpiece was inspired by Peter Paul Rubens's *Consequences of War* (1638–39)—with perfectly marmoreal bodies over which his revolutionaries clamber—but it was based on real events. He began it shortly after witnessing open warfare on the streets of Paris and finished the eleven-foot canvas several months later, in time to display it at the official 1831 Salon. Delacroix's exalted depiction of a bayonet-wielding, flag-bearing, semi-naked Amazon is not that of a historical individual. Instead, the figure serves as an allegory of Liberty, plumped by the raptures of romantic aesthetic and political ideals. The monumental canvas has drawn comparisons with the figure towering over New York Harbor, *Liberty Enlightening the World*—designed by Frédéric-Auguste Bartholdi and gifted by the French people to the United States in 1886.

Delacroix portrays Liberty's handsome head in profile, like a monarch on a coin; atop she wears the Phrygian cap, or *bonnet rouge*, a symbol of freedom that is echoed by the ubiquitous image of Malcolm X on T-shirts today. Surrounding her secular highness are several stock characters: a grimy-faced factory worker holding an infantry saber (leftover perhaps from a previous war); a fancy-pants bohemian sporting a hunting rifle; and a schoolboy brandishing two pistols. The painting's not-so-subtle message is that anyone can become a revolutionary. The rub is that Delacroix's epic scenario is humanly possible only in *Les Mis*.

Corresponding with his brother about his ambitions for the picture, Delacroix enthused: "I have undertaken a modern subject, a barricade, and although I may not have fought for my country, at least I shall have painted for her." The Frenchman created a heroic fantasy of egalitarian revolution. Myriad imitations have littered the world ever since.

3   J. M. W. Turner   *Slave Ship (Slavers Throwing Overboard the Dead and the Dying. Typhoon Coming On)* (1840)

Joseph Mallord William Turner (1775–1851) was a master painter of the sublime. A pioneer in the study of light, color, and atmosphere, he had a singular ability to depict dread, danger, awe, and terror.

The best advanced art has condemned barbarism for centuries.

In March 1877, the *Boston Evening Transcript* commented on one particularly committed painting: "Turner's *Slave Ship* is a picture of moans and tears and groans and shrieks. Every tint and shade and line throb with death and terror and blood. It is the embodiment of a giant protest, a mighty voice crying out against human oppression."

J. M. W. Turner painted *Slave Ship* in 1840 as an abolitionist protest, hoping it would catch the attention of Prince Albert when he attended the British Anti-slavery Conference (after the Slavery Abolition Act of 1833, British activists worked to outlaw the trade worldwide). Instead, it caught the eye of critic John Ruskin, its first owner, who in his 1843 book *Modern Painters* pronounced it a masterpiece: "If I were reduced to rest Turner's immortality upon any single work, I should choose this." Ruskin and others saw in the composition fearful echoes of one of the most shameful episodes in British history—the true story of the slave ship *Zong*.

The *Zong* took off from the coast of Africa in 1781, loaded to the rafters with human cargo. After veering off course and running short of water, its captain and crew threw 133 men, women, and children into the Caribbean Sea. Their logic was wolfishly mercantile: if slaves drowned rather than died of thirst, the slavers could collect insurance on the cargo. When abolitionists tried to bring criminal charges, the solicitor general rejected their plea: no "human people" had been jettisoned, he claimed, "the case is the same as if wood had been thrown overboard."

From this disgraceful episode, Turner conjured a vision of universal rage: a scenario in which, according to Ruskin, "the fire of the sunset falls along the trough of the sea, dyeing it with an awful but glorious light, the intense and lurid splendor which burns like gold and bathes like blood." A single glance at the painting reveals the spectacle of awesome nature unchained and an atmosphere as terrifying as any in footage of the Twin Towers in flames on 9/11.

Often called simply *Slave Ship*, the picture shows a three-master with its sails down being tossed around in the storm like a toy. In the foreground, arms and legs with chains attached emerge from the water— chum to be devoured by toothy sea creatures. The sun glowers over the tumultuous proceedings like a giant apparition. Shining vertically, its fulgurant rays thrust a dagger into the heart of the red-brown sea.

Nearly eighty years after Turner's depiction of human violence, W. B. Yeats composed a poetic analogue: "The blood-dimmed tide is loosed, and everywhere / The ceremony of innocence is drowned; / The best lack all conviction, while the worst / Are full of passionate intensity."

Gustave
Courbet

The Stone Breakers
(1849)

Gustave Courbet (1819–1877) was among the first artists to embody the avant-garde ideal: he was at once a man of his time and at odds with it. *The Stone Breakers* was the first of his great works. It was destroyed in the bombing of Dresden in 1945, whereupon it joined the Colossus of Rhodes and the Buddhas of Bamiyan on a list of lost treasures.

Painted just a year after the February Revolution and Karl Marx and Friedrich Engels penned *The Communist Manifesto*, Gustave Courbet's *The Stone Breakers* depicted workers doing the grunt work that industrial-age machines would soon take on. Inspired by a scene Courbet witnessed of two men crushing rocks for gravel—one of the most backbreaking and worst-paid jobs imaginable—the artist rendered his figures monumental and faceless. For the author of "The Realist Manifesto," the picture relayed life as lived by millions of downtrodden laborers: relentless poverty taken straight, no chaser.

Courbet's commitment to real life consumed him. In an era when idealization and sentimentality dominated the Salon—these traits were often what made a picture "art"—he rebelled against the academy's preferences in order to accurately reflect the times he lived in. In 1848, French workers also rebelled, but against the state. Though Courbet did not man the barricades, he turned his political sympathies epic.

Consider the extra-large proportions of Courbet's masterpiece. Tapestry-sized, it related to the solemnity and orthodoxy with which classical themes were traditionally treated. It frustrated received tastes, chiefly by presenting members of society's lowest ranks in place of emperors and nymphs. Rather than swords, it features pickaxes; instead of grandees in rich vestments, plebes in tattered work clothes; in place of saintly sandals, heavy clogs.

The supersizing of Courbet's peasants did not heroize them, however. By accumulating copious concrete detail the way Gustave Flaubert did, the artist advanced "the most complete expression of poverty." The two figures, for instance, are ill-suited to such grueling labor: the kneeling man is too old and the straining boy too young. Their struggle for survival was fairly typical for mid-nineteenth-century rural France.

Courbet's narrative and formal choices are intimately connected. His pictures are propelled by rough brushwork, which led critics to claim that he painted like someone waxing boots. Rather than engage the highly polished, refined style of the era, the artist cultivated a deliberately unfinished look, the better to convey his figures' punishing work and dreary setting. He also refused to focus on the elements of a picture that usually received the lion's share of attention. Unlike most nineteenth-century academic painters, he often ignored hands and faces to lavish care on a ripped shirt, patched pants, or stray rocks. It's precisely these details that made Courbet's *The Stone Breakers* appear so grittily real.

Honoré
Daumier

The Third-Class Carriage
(c. 1862–64)

In 1832, Honoré Daumier (1808–1879) was condemned to a six-month prison term for the publication of a caricature that portrayed King Louis-Philippe as Gargantua, François Rabelais's gluttonous giant. The Jon Stewart of French caricature, he routinely satirized France's bourgeoisie and the justice system, and exposed the misery that the urban poor went through during industrialization.

Honoré Daumier was many things—a prolific printmaker, painter, and sculptor, and an acerbic commentator on life in France as it entered the industrial age. Baptized the "Michelangelo of caricature" by his contemporary Honoré de Balzac—the wellspring of French realism—Daumier was the pest that gave the powerful classes heaving conniptions. The words the critic Robert Hughes used to describe Goya apply equally well to the Frenchman. He too was "a merciless critic of the society around him and a habitual protester against war, cruelty, and the violence of unjust authority."

But not every arrow in the artist's quiver was tipped with satire. Besides pinpointing the rapacity of the rich, the vanity of bluebloods, and the not infrequent stupidity of power, Daumier also produced insightful and sympathetic portraits of his fellow *citoyens*. His best and most celebrated depiction of France's lower classes is this unfinished oil painting of a group of worn-out workers traveling in a cramped and gloomy third-class carriage. The picture does double duty as both a keen-eyed family portrait and a documentary image.

The railroad was the subject of several of Daumier's canvases—it was the commuter conveyance that defined industrialization. Its cars ferried laborers to factories and enabled peasants to migrate to cities in search of work. Ex-croppers sought to maximize their job prospects; others fled a dying way of life that promised only hunger, misery, and exploitation. It is possible to hazard a guess as to which outlook fits the family depicted in *The Third-Class Carriage*. Daumier's picture features the human life cycle: an infant, a mother, a grandmother, and a boy, but no adult male. The scenario suggests that the primary breadwinner is absent and the family has tumbled precipitously on its luck. The underprivileged are not idealized, like representations of the Holy Family, but are shown to be shabby, dirty, and exhausted.

Daumier describes one poor household's passage to their next station in life. What awaits them in Paris is not a step up, but overcrowded housing, unsanitary conditions, and continued hardship.

Édouard Manet

The Execution of Emperor Maximilian (1868–69)

Édouard Manet (1832–1883) is widely considered the heir to the phrase coined by Charles Baudelaire: "the painter of modern life." His groundbreaking works portray the transition to modernity in the nineteenth century. Of Manet's political painting, curator John Elderfield writes, "Political art . . . does not reduce human affairs to slogans; it complicates rather than simplifies."

Journalism, declared Philip Graham, former publisher of *The Washington Post*, in 1963, "is the first rough draft of history." In art, however, things had already gone further: when the painter Édouard Manet tackled history, his works were not only rough drafts but final drafts.

Manet set the standard for painting contemporary subjects that bristled with authenticity. Among his controversial subjects—of which there were many, including the depiction of a mousy prostitute *as a prostitute*—one proved especially radical politically: the 1867 death by firing squad of the Austrian Archduke Ferdinand Maximilian.

Installed as a puppet emperor in Mexico in 1863 by Napoleon III, Maximilian depended entirely on the presence of the French army to maintain power; when Napoleon's troops withdrew, he was overrun by Republican forces and captured. On June 19, 1867, he was executed, alongside two local generals in the manner of Christ and the two thieves. These events unleashed the nineteenth-century equivalent of a media frenzy—complete with eyewitness accounts, photographs, and prints.

Manet recognized a great opportunity when he stumbled on one. He had recently seen Goya's *The Third of May 1808* (1814) at the Prado in Madrid, the first great modern painting about death by fusillade (compare it to Hans Memling's bow-and-arrow execution in his *Martyrdom of Saint Sebastian*, c. 1475). Mexico's regicide provided a clean sweep: the French artist could tackle the fustiness of history painting, the conservatism of the Paris Salon (which, predictably, rejected his final canvas), and Napoleon III's authoritarianism.

Manet started painting the execution in 1867. Two versions are either fragmentary or incomplete: the first is at the Museum of Fine Arts, Boston, and the second is at the National Gallery in London. The third painting, on your left, is in the collection of Kunsthalle Mannheim in Germany and has its i's dotted and its t's crossed. This was the only version to be exhibited in public during the artist's lifetime. In 1879, it was shipped to New York and then Boston and billed as a public attraction, with viewers being charged twenty-five cents for the privilege. The enterprise was a fiasco. Eventually, the three compositions were mothballed in the artist's Paris studio; not until the early twentieth century would the turn to realism cause them to be rescued from oblivion.

An astounding depiction of the execution post-factum, the Mannheim painting casts the viewer in the role of a rubbernecker watching a firing squad: the triggers have just been pulled, the oaths shouted, the rifle smoke has yet to clear. One of Maximilian's dark-skinned generals rears back with arms raised (the pose is lifted from Goya's picture); the second awaits his bullet with hands crossed in a pose of beatitude. Maximilian, for his part, couldn't look more surprised. Death has found him just as life, and thus Manet portrayed him: gullible, wide-eyed, and unprepared.

Käthe
Kollwitz

Memorial Sheet for
Karl Liebknecht
(1920)

DiE LEBENDEN DEM TOTEN . ERiNNERUNG AN DEN 15. JANUAR 1919

Käthe Kollwitz (1867–1945) was the first woman to be admitted
into the Prussian Academy of Arts in 1919. Her concertedly
political art reached wide audiences during her lifetime through
her use of newspapers, posters, and prints. In 1937, the Nazis
included her work in their *Degenerate Art* exhibition. *Pietà*, a
large-scale model of her sculpture *Mother with Her Dead Son*,
was made for the Central Memorial of the Federal Republic of
Germany for the Victims of War and Dictatorship in Berlin in
1993. The sculpture's appropriateness has been hotly debated
ever since.

Käthe Kollwitz was rarely wrong about suffering. Having lost her younger son in World War I, Kollwitz kept a studio in her husband's medical clinic, surrounded by needy patients. Life in Germany between the wars presented a daily litany of challenges. The founding of the country's Weimar Republic, in 1919, ushered in a period of social and political unrest. That same year, the Communist Party staged an armed uprising in Berlin. After the violent suppression of the revolt, its leaders, Karl Liebknecht and Rosa Luxemburg, were murdered while in the custody of right-wing paramilitaries.

Though not a communist, Kollwitz sympathized with the outpouring of grief among workers for the loss of their leaders. She also strongly identified with the loss suffered by the Liebknecht family. When they asked her to commemorate the Communist leader on his funeral bier, the artist accepted immediately. She soon realized that she needed an extra flash of inspiration to transform her conventional mortuary drawing into the powerful print you see to the left.

Kollwitz had abandoned painting for drawing early in her career. She turned to printmaking to popularize her images of working-class subjects. While experimenting with Liebknecht's memorial, Kollwitz attended an exhibition of woodcuts by the sculptor and printmaker Ernst Barlach. The elemental rawness of his woodcuts proved a revelation—their rough edges and stark black-and-white contrasts "knocked me over," she said, and presented a way of tapping into the collective anguish surrounding Liebknecht's political martyrdom.

Kollwitz's *Memorial* draws on centuries of religious painting. Ironically, it casts the atheist leader as a Christ figure, yet the composition is largely devoted to the mourners. A woman holds a baby over the heads of others; a pair of bright faces among a mass of darkened male miens, the two figures propose a life-affirming counterpart to the victim's death—and imply a conciliatory alternative to the ongoing spiral of violence.

Kollwitz was adamant about her freedom of expression and her ambivalent support for an apostle of violent revolution. In her diary she wrote: "As an artist, I have the right to extract the emotional content from everything, to let it make an impression on me and to express it externally. So I also have the right to represent the workers' farewell to Liebknecht, even to dedicate it to the workers, without thereby following Liebknecht politically. Or not?!"

Vladimir
Tatlin

*Monument to the
Third International*
(1920)

A painter, sculptor, and architect, Vladimir Tatlin (1885–1953) was
a founder of the constructivist movement, an arch-propagandist
for the Soviet state, and the designer of the world's greatest unbuilt
monument. His design for *Letatlin* (1929–32), a futuristic glider
that resembled a giant insect, never achieved flight. After falling
out of favor with the authorities, he died in obscurity in Moscow.

Imagine being asked to design a monument to the future with only a few sticks of wood and a roll of chicken wire.

This was Vladimir Tatlin's dilemma when Vladimir Lenin, leader of the fledgling Soviet Union, charged him with implementing a brazenly doctrinal plan for producing "Monumental Propaganda"—a campaign to remove tsarist monuments and replace them with Bolshevik slabs, which would, in time, make America's push to rid itself of odious Confederate-era statues look, well, like a Russian tea party.

Tatlin's response to his mission had two phases. He took stock of the overwhelming number of figurative sculptures already adorning the Soviet Union's squares. Then, firm in his belief that the future demanded a resolutely abstract look, he proposed a spectacularly unrealizable monument: a 1,300-foot corkscrewing paean to metal girder construction and avant-garde utopias—equal parts Eiffel Tower and Leaning Tower of Pisa. Modeled with little more than hobbyist tools, *Monument to the Third International* ran up against the impoverished reality of 1920s Russia. Chronic shortages of money and materials meant the idealistic project was impossible to complete.

If built, Tatlin's monument would have immediately earned the Soviet Union bragging rights for the world's tallest building. Made from glass and steel, it would have stacked four transparent spaces on top of each other—a cube, a pyramid, a cylinder, and a half sphere. These enclosures were intended to house the Comintern (communism's short-lived international governing body), several branches of the Russian government, and a radio tower. To this Tatlin added one more far-fetched twist. Each of the four glass structures was to revolve at different but complementary speeds.

Leon Trotsky thought the proposal looked like "unremoved scaffolding," but generations of artists, architects, writers, and dreamers would admire its soaring ingenuity; the poet Vladimir Mayakovsky, for example, called it "the first Russian monument without a beard." Like Thomas More's *Utopia*—named after an ancient Greek word that means "nowhere" or "no place"—Tatlin's monument to the future was never really intended to reach the construction stage. As such, his preposterous tower is the forerunner of Che Guevara's famous dictum a half-century later: "Be realistic, demand the impossible."

George Grosz *Ecce Homo* (1922–23)

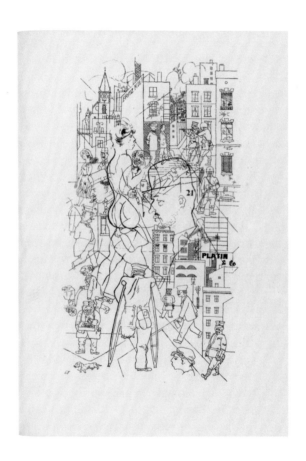

When George Grosz (1893–1959) titled his most important artwork *Ecce Homo*, he spared no one, least of all himself, in his composite view of social decay. In his autobiography, *A Little Yes and a Big No*, the artist reflected on life in Berlin in the 1920s: "I was each one of the very characters I drew, the champagne-swilling glutton favored by fate no less than the poor beggar standing with outstretched hands in the rain. I was split in two, just like society at large."

Here's an idea to chew on during your next museum visit: things that are bad for society are sometimes good for artists.

This, in any event, appeared to be the case for German artist George Grosz. After serving two stints in the army during World War I, Grosz returned to a homeland transformed by vice, sexual permissiveness, hyperinflation, barricades, and political assassinations. The place was, by turns, dangerous and electric. That tension became Grosz's inkwell of hydrochloric acid, from which flowed a torrent of satirical drawings, paintings, watercolors, and prints.

In time, Grosz decanted this outpouring into a portfolio of prints titled *Ecce Homo*, after a book by Friedrich Nietzsche (and the words uttered by Pontius Pilate when presenting the scourged Christ to the mob before his crucifixion). Grosz printed ten thousand copies of an especially unruly batch of one hundred caricatures. These were made up of sixteen scathingly original watercolors and eighty-four scabrous pen-and-ink drawings.

Grosz's book savages life in postwar Germany. Its pages are chock-full of politicians, businessmen, prostitutes, winos, tramps, and wounded veterans, cavorting wildly in imitation of their real-life counterparts. Official reaction to the prints was swift: the German government banned the portfolio, and Grosz was put on trial for "offences against public morality and for besmirching the values of the German people." Soon after, the artist was sued for slander by the army; he settled damages of six thousand marks and was forced to remove twenty-two of the portfolio's offending plates.

Unbowed, Grosz continued his crusade against censorship, official notions of degeneracy, and craven political mores. On relocating to New York in 1932, he evaluated his legacy: "My drawings will naturally stay true—they are fireproof. They will later be seen as Goya's work [is]. They are not documents of the class struggle, but eternally living documents of human stupidity and brutality." When the Nazis took power a year later, 285 of his works were pulled from public collections and destroyed; others were included, predictably, in the Nazi Party's *Degenerate Art* exhibition.

Querschnitt (which translates as "cross section"), at left, is a perfect example of Grosz's dynamic depiction of the chronic political turmoil in postwar Germany. The lithograph translates into form the method he and fellow Berlin Dadaist John Heartfield dubbed "photomontage" and overlaps vignettes of hustling, profiteering, and public executions, among other toxic activities, capturing the experience of living through a slow-motion civil war better than any single photograph could. Per Grosz's print, Germany was all bourgeois decadence, prostitution, indigence, and political violence, with Berlin its crowded and immoral capital.

Not infrequently, artistic milieus are also sheer hell. To quote filmmaker John Waters on New York in the 1970s: "It's always right before a storm that the air is filled with dangerous possibilities."

Max Beckmann

Departure
(1932–35)

Max Beckmann (1884–1950) was the epitome of the artist in exile. He fled Nazi Germany for the Netherlands in 1937, where he continued to make paintings that channeled personal experience in the service of a political worldview. In 1947, he emigrated to America and taught art in Saint Louis and New York. Although he spent just three years in the US, his influence on generations of American painters has been incalculable.

When history jumps the track, artworks like the painting on your left take courage.

Max Beckmann suffered the first public attacks on his art by the Nazi press in 1931, two years before the party achieved power. When Adolf Hitler was declared chancellor, in 1933, the artist was dismissed from his teaching post in Frankfurt and the barrage of criticism steadily grew. By the time the Nazis marched their "blood and soil" madness into Germany's museums, Beckmann's reputation as a pioneering modern painter had been savaged.

Beckmann left Frankfurt for Berlin in 1936. That year, the Führer doubled down on his campaign to wipe out "cultural Bolshevism" in Germany. One of his first steps was to confiscate nearly six hundred works by Beckmann—among them paintings, watercolors, drawings, and prints—from German museums. The day after the *Degenerate Art* exhibition opened in Munich, in 1937, Beckmann fled Germany—but not before unburdening himself of this spectacular triptych, long considered to be the painter's masterpiece.

Departure at once attracts and repels associations, like a magnet. The trio of canvases shuffles figures and objects drawn from literature, art, and mythology together with personal and political symbols. The central image of a seaborne fisher king and his family is flanked by two canvases that feature trapped and tortured figures. Though Beckmann consistently denied that *Departure* could be boiled down to a single political idea, his triptych is rightly seen as an explicit response to the abuses of Hitler's fascist regime.

How else to read the sadism inflicted on the figures in the left-hand panel—a weeping man has stumps for arms, a woman is bound at her hands and feet and made to stare at a newspaper—or the right-hand panel's robed Lady Liberty carrying a lamp? As opposed to Delacroix's *Liberty Leading the People* (1830) or the Statue of Liberty, Beckmann's depiction of this icon of freedom is literally weighed down by a dead body. With European civilization on the cusp of disaster, Beckmann painted the corpse upside-down.

From Hitler's rise to power to the end of World War II, Beckmann painted like a man possessed. Contrary to expectation, he didn't just paint about suffering and despair. About *Departure*'s center panel, which he optimistically pegged *The Homecoming*, he declared: "The Queen carries the greatest treasure—Freedom—as her child in her lap. Freedom is the one thing that matters—it is the departure, the new start."

11   Walker Evans   *Bud Fields and His Family,*
Hale County, Alabama
(1936, published 1941)

Walker Evans (1903–1975) was a champion of photographic
candor. His refusal to romanticize poverty and his commitment
to approach his subjects forthrightly redefined the medium.
Among the artists Evans inspired were Helen Levitt, Robert
Frank, Diane Arbus, Lee Friedlander, Bernd and Hilla Becher,
and the conceptualist Sherrie Levine, who rephotographed
his Depression-era pictures for a series entitled *After Walker
Evans* (1981).

This photograph is more shocking today than when it was first made.

A picture of destitution sporting a white face, it challenges the viewer with brutal honesty that outstrips other images of indigence across the ages—from Velazquez's painting of a ragged water seller in Seville (1618–22) to Van Gogh's portrait of a Dutch family, *The Potato Eaters* (1885). In our time, economic suffering is usually associated with skin colors other than white, nationalities other than American. Walker Evans's print relays an unvarnished truth that has long made millions of privileged people blanch: poverty, like profiteering, can be brutally color-blind.

Transparent, clinical, unheroic. That was the look Walker Evans worked hard to achieve as a photographer, from the year he signed up with Franklin D. Roosevelt's Farm Security Administration to the day in 1936 when he was hired, along with writer James Agee, to travel down south to chronicle the hardscrabble lives of Alabama tenant farmers. The story, contracted by *Fortune* magazine, never saw the light of day (Agee refused all edits). Instead, it was published in 1941 in expanded book form as *Let Us Now Praise Famous Men*. This iconic collaboration contains Agee's plaintive text and thirty-one no-nonsense black-and-white photographs by Evans.

Working with a large-format eight-by-ten camera, Evans captured his subjects with puritanical precision and a Spartan economy of means. His framing and composition are straightforward. In this photo of Bud Fields and his family, three adults sit on chairs and a stained mattress with two children and a baby in a wooden shack. They are dirty and barefoot. The young boy at the center of the picture is naked from the waist down. The father, behind him, is shirtless, except for a patterned kerchief. Slung over his right shoulder, the cloth is delicately placed to hide his skin cancer.

Evans's artistic goal was to create "pure records" of American life. His frank photograph of the Fields clan communicates, years hence, the family's stoicism while also asserting the power of the plain, unadorned photograph.

"There is no way in the world that anyone could sit down and convey to you what the times were really like back then," said Irving Fields, grandson of Bud Fields, in *Fortune* in 2005—the gulf between his experience and that of his ancestors was vast. But one surefire way to dispatch those felt facts has existed since 1936, the year the photograph of the Fields family was taken (the image was first printed in 1941). It's all there, chapter and verse, in Evans's picture.

12   Pablo Picasso   *Guernica* (1937)

The figure of Pablo Picasso (1881–1973) dominates Western culture. No painter, before or since, has been as celebrated in his own lifetime. The paragon of the modernist protean genius, the Spaniard's reputation has outlasted even the postmodern condemnations of proteanism and genius. Picasso remains one of the few creators with whom all living artists have to reckon today—whether they want to or not.

As the end of World War II approached, Pablo Picasso took stock of what he had learned about the relationship between art and politics. Then, he penned a mini-manifesto. "Painting is not made to decorate apartments," he declared. "It's an offensive and defensive weapon against the enemy."

In the mid-1930s, Picasso had been promoting himself chiefly as a cruel intimist, a conjurer of cramped, claustrophobic interior spaces, a creator of nightmarishly sexualized sculptures and pictures rendered in geometric or bulbous forms. After the opening of the World's Fair in Paris in 1937, the celebrated Spaniard acquired a status much more exalted than that of modern painting's *dévastateur* of the bedchamber. After the figurative and literal fog of war cleared, he would be recognized as the genius who created the century's greatest work of antiwar art.

Guernica is a memorial to the Nazi aerial bombing of the ancient Basque town of the same name. It represents the opposite of a heroic memorial; it is, instead, the world's first anti-monument. The painting is dedicated not to destruction and despair but to denouncing what the poet Robert Burns referred to as "man's inhumanity to man."

Measuring eleven and a half by twenty-five and a half feet, it is permanently located in room 206 on the second floor of Madrid's Museo Nacional Centro de Arte Reina Sofía, surrounded by galleries containing other Picasso works from the 1930s and 1940s and a scale model of the Spanish Pavilion designed by Josep Lluís Sert from the World's Fair—the painting's first home before it was sent on a fifty-four-year tour that included stops at the Whitechapel Gallery in London, the Sao Paulo Biennial, The Museum of Modern Art in New York, and the Prado in Madrid.

Guernica is an enveloping, movie-screen-sized scene of human agony, pleading, and disorientation painted in luminous black and white. Picasso prepared his giant canvas with lead white, graphite, and finely ground glass for a supremely radiant effect; as such, it still proves a shock to most viewers. A room is being ripped apart by a bomb—bodies are weaponized, figures sprout projectile tears, and beasts brandish swords for tongues. The image is "the *Last Judgement* of our age," said curator Charles Lindstrom. As a verdict, it is renewed by every fresh outbreak of senseless violence and chaos: from the slaughter of civilians in Syria to ISIS-inspired attacks in Europe and North America to the mass shooting in Las Vegas.

13   José Clemente   *Carnival of Ideologies*
      Orozco   (1937–39)

The influence of José Clemente Orozco (1883–1949) can
be traced to the American painters Thomas Hart Benton,
Jackson Pollock, and Jacob Lawrence, and the Chicano mural
movement. The artist's frequent travels across the US-Mexico
border to paint murals in California, New York, and New
Hampshire prefigure the movement of millions of migrants
from Mexico and Central America.

About his autobiography, published in 1945, José Clemente Orozco was laconic: "There is nothing of special interest in it, no famous exploits or heroic deeds, no extraordinary or miraculous happenings." But the artist's coruscating irony cannot minimize the achievements contained in his great political mural *Carnival of Ideologies*.

Part of a fresco cycle that the Mexican muralist painted inside the stairwell of the Governor's Palace in the city of Guadalajara, the soaring composition depicts a time not unlike ours, where opposing ideas of left, right, and center inspire a vision of global politics as World Wrestling Entertainment. Forget about secular saints Nelson Mandela and Abraham Lincoln when considering this picture; think instead of Donald "Cheeto-in-Chief" Trump and "Rocket Man" Kim Jong-Un.

Like the packed panoramas of his fellow muralists Diego Rivera and David Alfaro Siqueiros (or looking back to the fevered vistas of Hieronymus Bosch), Orozco's mural teems with so much information that it needs itemizing to unpack the ideas contained within. The fresco's ceiling and side panels, for instance, are chock-full of individual figures that coalesce into anonymous masses. Few modern-age frescoes, in fact, invite as much consideration of sweeping historical processes and the collateral human damage they engender.

Orozco's central ceiling panel features a massive Father Miguel Hidalgo—the Roman Catholic priest is considered the progenitor of Mexico's War of Independence—setting fire to world revolution. Directly below him, hordes of men massacre each other pitilessly while, on one of the mural's flanges, an ocean of humanity engages in a pitched, bone-crushing battle. The artist achieves an explosive dynamism with a stingy palette of black, white, orange, and red. The fresco's ideological agnosticism is another stroke of genius: its figures wield a confusion of political symbols that include swastikas, crosses, and Phrygian caps as well as hammers and sickles.

In Orozco's mind, left- and right-wing ideologies were interchangeable. This was a personal conclusion he drew from having slogged through ten years of the Mexican Revolution. In his autobiography, Orozco characterized the decade after 1910 thusly: "People grew used to killing, to the most pitiless egotism, to naked bestiality . . . In the world of politics it was the same, war without quarter, struggle for power and wealth . . . Underneath it all, subterranean intrigues went on among the friends of today and the enemies of tomorrow, resolved, when the time came, upon mutual extermination."

While it may seem strange to select an artwork that is skeptical of ideology for this book, Orozco's hard-won freethinking constitutes a crucial kind of political stance.

Jacob
      Lawrence

The Migration Series
(1940–41)

Jacob Lawrence (1917–2000) called his pared-down painting
style "dynamic cubism." Despite the artist's debt to synthetic
cubism and Henri Matisse's flat forms, his greatest triumph
was in achieving a demotic form that channels the plain shapes
and colors of black Americans' experience during the mid-
twentieth century.

The subject was gargantuan.

The Great Migration was, simply, the biggest internal migration of people in American history—in the words of Henry Louis Gates Jr., it was "the largest movement of black bodies since slavery." Between 1916 and 1970, six million African Americans moved from the rural South to the cities of the Northeast, Midwest, and West; nonetheless, the epic event garnered no official monument, no *Grapes of Wrath*, no ABC miniseries, and, to date, no museum marking this exodus of the industrial age.

Black America's flight into the northern wilderness during the first decades of the twentieth century was memorialized instead in a series of sixty modestly sized paintings on store-bought panels by a then unknown black artist named Jacob Lawrence. At twenty-one, he was hired as a painter for the Federal Arts Project, which was part of Franklin D. Roosevelt's Works Progress Administration. In his own words, though, he was "too young for a wall."

Born in Atlantic City, New Jersey, to parents who had fled poverty and the Jim Crow crimes of the South, Lawrence settled in Harlem, New York, just as the clash of rural migration and urban culture was producing the rich cultural synthesis that became known as the Harlem Renaissance. Years later, Lawrence told an interviewer: "I am the black community." It was not so much a boast as a statement of fully immersed fact.

Already steeped in the culture and stories of the migration, Lawrence tackled his enormous subject by conducting research at the New York Public Library's Schomburg Center, the city's chief repository of African American history. When he put brush to panel, he worked from pencil drawings and narrative captions that he prepared for each vignette using only quick-drying tempera in a limited range of colors (blue-green, orange, yellow, and gray-brown). The final result, according to the artist, made up "one work, not sixty works."

As unified as any Diego Rivera mural, Lawrence's portable masterpiece compressed, in the manner of a Mississippi John Hurt ballad, an entire history of collective hardship—floods, lynchings, labor camps, race riots, mass migration—into threescore paintings of no more than twelve by eighteen inches. In each panel, the subject is stripped to its essential expression: in a panel captioned *They were very poor*, a faceless man and woman stare down at empty bowls; another, called *One of the largest race riots occurred in East St. Louis*, features a tangle of arms, legs, feet, fists, and knives.

The first half of Lawrence's series is devoted to the social injustices and economic hardships of the South, while the second half describes the life migrants found when they arrived in the North. The work is bookended by a pair of railroad station pictures. Panel 1 depicts a crowd pushing toward ticket windows marked CHICAGO, NEW YORK, and ST. LOUIS. Panel 60, the last work, describes a mass of figures packed shoulder to shoulder on a railroad platform. It's simply captioned *And the migrants kept coming*.

Robert
Motherwell   *Elegy to the Spanish
Republic No. 70
(1961)*

Robert Motherwell (1915–1991) was that rare thing in 1950s
America: a painter who was also an intellectual. He read widely,
studied at Stanford, Harvard, and Columbia, and spoke enough
French to befriend the surrealists. A painter widely associated
with the triumph of abstract expressionism, he once described
himself as belonging to "a family of 'black' painters and earth
color painters in masses, which would include Manet and Goya
and Matisse."

This epic work had a modest beginning. Initially inspired by an eight-by-ten-inch pen-and-ink sketch Robert Motherwell titled *Elegy to the Spanish Republic No. 1* (1948), this heroic paint-on-canvas variation constitutes one of the world's most poignant meditations on sex, death, and the tragedy of life itself.

The first of more than two hundred *Elegies to the Spanish Republic* that Motherwell created, the drawing was made to accompany a perfectly apolitical poem by his friend, the critic Harold Rosenberg. What followed that small work on paper was a cascade of giant black ovoids and thick vertical bands that the artist set dramatically against contrasting white backgrounds. Titled in homage to Picasso's *Guernica* (1937), Goya's *The Disasters of War* (1810–20), and the memory of the murdered poet Federico García Lorca, Motherwell's series of monochrome shapes were marshaled to access both a core set of liberal ideals and what the painter once described as "a world of feeling."

Motherwell had not been to Spain before starting his Spanish *Elegies*. Nonetheless, he hitched his cycle of repeating monumental abstract forms to the tragedy of that country's civil war. The three-year conflict caused more than five hundred thousand deaths; it also occasioned the first aerial bombings of civilians in history—both of which roused many artists and writers to respond. By the time Motherwell started to paint his *Elegies*, the Spanish Civil War was well on its way to becoming what it would remain in the collective psyche: metaphorical shorthand for human suffering and injustice everywhere.

With *Elegy to the Spanish Republic No. 70*, as with the related works in the series, Motherwell took a page from the symbolist poet Stéphane Mallarmé. A plastic interpretation of the French radical's literary maxim that correspondences exist between things that are more emotional than factual, the painting establishes a set of tensions that pit areas of contrasting light (vitality) against areas of shadow (death), and thick bands of descending black paint against floating, bulbous charcoal shapes. These ominous, cloudy forms suggest warring abstract mythological forces but also images of portentous specificity—falling bombs and their blackened trajectory; the patent leather hats of Spain's notorious Guardia Civil; a bull's pizzle and a pair of scissored testicles.

In keeping with his contention that his work was not directly political, Motherwell always maintained that the real subject of this and other *Elegies* was a general meditation on life and death. Stark, funereal, and as nightmarish as a reading of Grimms' *Fairy Tales* with a Castilian lisp, this painting presents a vision of trauma that is dark, monumental, and pregnant with uneasy associations.

Robert Rauschenberg *Retroactive I* (1963)

Some artists leave a mark; only a handful deliver the kind of legacy handed down by Robert Rauschenberg (1925–2008), the art gospel–spreading, medium-challenging, style-switching Johnny Appleseed. Rauschenberg was making groundbreaking artwork in New York City by the age of twenty-five. By the time the polymath died in his artistic idyll of Captiva Island, Florida, he had anticipated just about every modern art movement and trend after abstract expressionism—from minimalism to conceptualism, from pop to performance, from serial collaborations to socially engaged art.

"I think a picture is more like the real world when it's made out of the real world."

These were words to live by for Robert Rauschenberg, a champion artistic innovator and virtuoso tinkerer in the vein of Leonardo da Vinci and Pablo Picasso. Spectacularly influential, Rauschenberg today is known for possessing an outsized vision. Yet only a few of his artworks possess the eagle-eyed intensity and anticipatory reach of *Retroactive I,* an elegy to America's thirty-fifth president, made after his assassination.

The oil and silk screen on canvas features an ethereal blue image of then Senator John F. Kennedy during his second presidential debate with Richard Nixon. Rauschenberg had transferred the celebrated photograph onto a silk screen only weeks before the magnicide, on November 22, 1963. After the assassination, Rauschenberg dallied, unsure as to whether he was fully in control of the late president's image, but finally pushed ahead with the picture.

Layered onto a virtual library of contemporaneous, art-historical, and ancient references, Rauschenberg's centrally placed Kennedy shares space with silk-screened reproductions of a NASA space suit, a glass of bilious green water, an upturned crate of apples, a black-and-white painted blob that resembles a darkening sun, and, finally, a time-lapse photo of naked ambulatory bodies that invokes both Marcel Duchamp's *Nude Descending a Staircase, No. 2* (1912) and Masaccio's grieving figures in *Expulsion of Adam and Eve from the Garden of Eden* (c. 1427). Before Rauschenberg, who knew artists could mash together footage from a 1960 CBS broadcast and visuals that recall Renaissance suffering?

Drawing from the real world and from the ubiquitous imagery of 1960s print and television, Rauschenberg fashioned a special kind of recombinant picture: one that makes perfectly quotidian images coexist not only with modern political tragedy but also with one of the most powerful symbols of loss known to Western art.

Andy Warhol *Orange Disaster #5*
(1963)

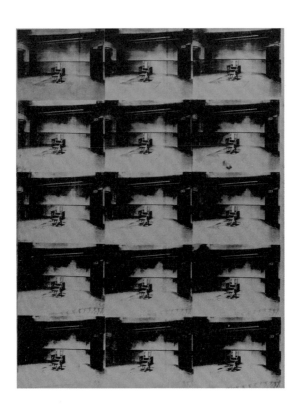

Andy Warhol (1928–1987) became the "King of Pop Art" by
trading older concerns, like the Depression-era fight for social
justice and the existential conceit of 1950s abstract expressionism,
for newly regnant postwar American phenomena such as celebrity
and advertising. Having started out as an illustrator, he wed
commercialism with fine art's social pretensions, going so far as
to say, "Being good in business is the best kind of art." Though
Warhol is famous for subjects such as Campbell's Soup cans,
Marilyn Monroe, and Elvis Presley, his greatest creation was
his own fame.

Suicides, car crashes, assassinations, race riots, and executions. These events, as well as their largely hapless and anonymous protagonists, were the flip side of the Hollywood-style fame Andy Warhol sought to capture in depictions of icons such as Elvis, Marlon Brando, Mao, and his ill-starred trio of 1960s demigoddesses—Marilyn Monroe, Elizabeth Taylor, and Jackie Kennedy.

Warhol christened these paintings his *Death and Disaster* series, in opposition to America's bubblegum dream of sunny celebrity. Of the hundreds of electric chair-themed works he made between 1962 and 1965, *Orange Disaster #5* is by far the most hair-raising. Stacked vertically, this flame-colored acrylic-on-canvas semaphore repeats over and over again— fifteen times to be exact—like a lurid nightmare.

In 1963, a year after Monroe's tragic passing from a barbiturate overdose, Warhol launched a suite of shocking new works using a stock image of the death chair. These canvases are marked by repeated mistakes: the result of slipped screens, drips, and uneven inkings. Executed by silk-screening black ink over "pretty" base hues—green, red, purple, yellow, orange, and the color that criminal psychologists call Drunk-Tank Pink—they show a single image of the government's high-voltage guillotine in various colors and sizes, reproduced serially with the enervating repetition of a sitcom trope.

The chair depicted in *Orange Disaster #5* is from a specific press photograph of the device used in the June 19, 1953, execution of Julius and Ethel Rosenberg, the American couple killed by the US government after their conviction for passing atomic secrets to Russia. But *Orange Disaster #5* doesn't feature the spies' likenesses. Instead, the painting portrays the solemn image of "Old Sparky"—as the prison's jailers christened the death machine. Pictured inside a cavernous chamber, the murderous contraption stands alone like an emancipated Hannibal Lecter, emboldened by one especially lapidary detail—a sign that reads SILENCE.

"When you see a gruesome picture over and over again," Warhol told the art critic Gene Swenson in 1963, "it doesn't really have any effect." But *Orange Disaster #5* contradicts this idea, both generally and in its particulars. If the painting's three rows of repeated images perfectly mimic the numbing reiteration of death in the modern media, Warhol's composition also dramatically emphasizes the electric chair's vacancy.

That emptiness is mesmerizing. The chair's repeated, acid-colored, mistake-prone image suggests a phenomenon that holds steady, from medieval depictions of the plague to videos of beheadings on the dark web—that the death of others is the ultimate form of voyeurism.

Ed Ruscha   *The Los Angeles County Museum on Fire* (1965–68)

The paintings of Ed Ruscha (b. 1937) can be read as both heroic and comical. A native of Omaha, Nebraska, he has produced some of the most iconic images of and about the "City of Angels." A master of wry cultural portraiture, he paints not so much things-in-the-world as things-turned-cultural-symbols, among which are prominent street signs, elliptical phrases in trompe l'oeil letters, and idealized mountain landscapes.

Think of Rome sacked by the Vandals. Of William Tecumseh Sherman's scorched-earth march on Atlanta. Of the Dresden bombing, the flattening of Hiroshima and Nagasaki, and the Twin Towers shot through and in flames. Ed Ruscha's painting *The Los Angeles County Museum on Fire* recalls all of these tragedies, but also their opposite. Like Samuel Beckett's *Molloy* and Terry Gilliam's movie *Brazil*, it flourishes at the intersection of tragedy and comedy.

Ruscha began his eleven-foot depiction of the Los Angeles County Museum of Art in the same year that it moved to a new complex near Hancock Park. Rendering its structures in precise detail, Ruscha portrays the museum with multiple vanishing points and from a slightly elevated perspective. Rather than describe the museum buildings with full realism, the artist presents them as an architect's model, without—among other practical details—ventilation ducts and other key features. The result is, like Hieronymus Bosch's *The Haywain Triptych* (c. 1512–15) or *The Simpsons'* "War of the Worlds"–inspired episode, a finely calibrated comic vision of a major social and cultural conflagration.

The flames engulfing the museum, however, evoke not an actual historical fire but the metaphorical blaze that engulfed both the city of Los Angeles and the United States during the mid-1960s. The assassination of John F. Kennedy, the increasing protests against American involvement in the Vietnam War, the racially restrictive covenants that ghettoized blacks and Mexican Americans—these were tinder for the inferno that was the Watts riots of 1965. The spark: a routine traffic stop that pitted an LAPD officer against a twenty-one-year-old African American man.

Although Ruscha's canvas—the largest he had painted to date— ostensibly delivers no moral verdict, it summons forth combustible forces that threaten civilization itself. The smoggily luminous painting pops the balloon on the museum's grandiose ambitions to propel Los Angeles into a first-tier cultural city. One can nearly hear the artist ask: "How is a place this bat-shit crazy supposed to play host to an encyclopedic museum?"

Joan Didion, for one, pegged Ruscha's Los Angeles perfectly during this period. "At the time of the 1965 Watts riots," she wrote in her barn burner of a book, *Slouching Towards Bethlehem*, "what struck the imagination most indelibly were the fires. For days one could drive the Harbor Freeway and see the city on fire, just as we had always known it would be in the end."

Grupo de
Artistas de
Vanguardia

Tucumán arde
(1968)

The Grupo de Artistas de Vanguardia (1966–68) included
Argentines such as León Ferrari, Graciela Carnevale, Norberto
Puzzolo, and Roberto Jacoby. They made a single artwork that
pushed political art to the breaking point. The choice thereafter:
make art or pick up a gun.

In 1968, a group of Argentine artists, journalists, and sociologists banded together to make the ultimate work of political art.

The Grupo de Artistas de Vanguardia formed in response to a series of national and international crises—the Vietnam War, student protests in Paris (as well as other cities in Europe and the Americas), the assassinations of Martin Luther King Jr. and Robert F. Kennedy, upheavals related to decolonization and the Cold War, and the repression and censorship of the military government of Juan Carlos Onganía. Their purpose: to turn art from something that hangs on the wall into a force that shakes the foundations of power.

The group first affiliated themselves with Argentina's largest labor union, the General Confederation of Labor (CGT). Next, they established a set of rules: avant-garde art would serve only the oppressed classes, instead of an elite public; art could no longer be shown in galleries or museums; real art would aspire to the status of political action.

The collective's manifesto, authored by artists María Teresa Gramuglio and Nicolás Rosa, declared the group's intention to "reveal the fallacious contradiction of the government and its supporting class"; they planned to achieve this through a series of events, interventions, and happenings. Their actions included a pair of exhibitions organized in the name of the millions of poor living in the region of Tucumán. The group's happenings received a fitting moniker—*Tucumán arde*, or "Tucumán Is Burning."

The group installed artworks at the CGT headquarters of two major cities, Rosario and Buenos Aires. Together with other left-leaning professionals, they took on the dictatorship's control directly. Many traveled to Tucumán for firsthand accounts of the impoverished conditions of Tucumeños. Others remained in Rosario and Buenos Aires to graffiti and paper over the streets with "counter-information" in imitation of clandestine political cadres.

In Rosario, the group combined a collage installation by León Ferrari with Walker Evans–style photographs of Tucumán's sugar-plantation workers and synoptic charts designed to demonstrate the links between mass misery and the corrupt government. They also produced audio and video recordings, slide shows, text pieces, a light work that flashed on and off to signal the scandalous frequency of infant mortality in the region, and a lengthy report on the root causes of Tucumán's poverty. In Rosario, the exhibition lasted two weeks. In Buenos Aires, the government shut it down after one day.

According to artist and writer Luis Camnitzer, *"Tucumán arde* was both a success and a failure"—chiefly in that art came up against the limits of nonviolent politics. The collective's members became targets of the military. A few went into exile. Others stopped making artwork and joined the guerilla movement. Several were "disappeared."

Art Workers'
Coalition

Q. And babies?
A. And babies.
(1969)

The Art Workers' Coalition (1969–71) was a loose-knit group
of artists and activists who pressured museums into addressing
social, cultural, and political issues. These issues included the
protection of free speech, greater representation for women and
minority creators, and an end to the Vietnam War.

The following is a partial transcript of a 1969 interview conducted by CBS reporter Mike Wallace with US Army Private Paul Meadlo, one of the American soldiers who participated in the My Lai massacre in 1968. The incident resulted in the deaths of 504 unarmed Vietnamese civilians.

Q: So you fired something like sixty-seven shots?
A: Right.
Q: And you killed how many at that time?
A: Well, I fired them automatic, so you can't . . . you just spray the area on them so you can't know how many you killed 'cause they were going fast. So I might have killed ten or fifteen of them.
Q: Men, women, and children?
A: Men, women, and children.
Q: And babies?
A: And babies.

That last question radicalized 1960s America. Among the people it mobilized were New York artists Irving Petlin, Jon Hendricks, and Frazer Dougherty of the Art Workers' Coalition (AWC). Together with members of The Museum of Modern Art's executive staff committee, they proposed the creation of a cosponsored, mass-produced poster as an expression of joint outrage at the massacre.

The idea was as simple as it was effective. Superimposed on a photograph by US combat photographer Ronald L. Haeberle of a dozen dead women and babies was Private Meadlo's chilling confession, printed in blood-red *New York Times* font.

Though MoMA initially agreed to fund and circulate the poster, the museum, to its everlasting shame, pulled its support after two of its trustees, New York governor Nelson Rockefeller and William S. Paley, opposed the initiative. Both were firm supporters of Richard Nixon's administration and fully backed the war effort. Paley, then president of MoMA's board and chairman of CBS, took on the role of museum spokesman. He refused to commit the museum to "any position on any matter not directly related to a specific function of the Museum."

No matter. The AWC, with the help of New York City's lithographers' union, printed fifty thousand copies. The posters were distributed both nationally and internationally by a grassroots network of artists, students, and peace activists. Images quickly circulated in newspapers and on television programs. Consumer versions papered the bedrooms of millions of America's youth. Carried in protest marches around the globe, the AWC's signature poster, like several other works in this book, became emblematic of antiwar sentiment and reappeared during various conflicts throughout history.

Later, in 1970, AWC members carried copies of the poster into MoMA and unfurled them in front of Picasso's *Guernica* (1937), then on loan to the museum. The confrontation of these works in one gallery rendered absurd the idea that *Q. And babies? A. And babies.* was too explicitly political to be exhibited inside the world's most important modern-art museum.

Cildo
Meireles

*Insertions into
Ideological Circuits:
Coca-Cola Project
(1970)*

A noted conceptualist, sculptor, and installation artist, Cildo
Meireles (b. 1948) is known for outfoxing the repressive machinery
of censorship to undermine the values of unfettered capitalism.
In North America and Europe, his work is often mistaken for a
tropical version of pop. In a 2014 interview, Meireles rejected this
spurious association. He was crystal clear: "Pop art is poison."

Can a Coke bottle carry a subversive message?

That question might have seemed absurd until 1970, when conceptualist Cildo Meireles launched his ongoing series *Insertions into Ideological Circuits*. Produced six years after a coup d'état deposed Brazil's democratically elected president João Goulart, Meireles's insurgent artworks spread underground messages while brilliantly (and bravely) skirting the censorship and violent repression meted out by a brutal military dictatorship.

If Italian curator Germano Celant's famous 1967 manifesto for arte povera was subtitled "Notes for a Guerrilla War," Meireles's artistic interventions (*intervençaos* in Portuguese) extended that struggle by confronting the Goliath of state power with found objects he weaponized like a twentieth-century David. Brazilian banknotes had their value changed to *zero cruzeiro* or were stamped with political slogans, such as "Who killed Herzog?" (The noted journalist Vladimir Herzog died in police custody under suspicious circumstances.) US bills underwent similar treatment.

Meireles's *Insertions into Ideological Circuits: Coca-Cola Project* proved the ideal vehicle to distribute these clandestine messages. Coca-Cola bottles were pitch-perfect symbols for global consumerism—and he inscribed them with gnomic missives before recycling them through a deposit system. The artist added questions, slogans, or illustrations to these charged receptacles in identical font.

Three key examples are pictured here: the bottles on the left and center read "Yankees go home!" while the one on the right bears an English-language description of Meireles's project: "To register informations [sic] and critical opinions on bottles and return them to circulation." Other bottles the artist put into circulation carried terse communications of a different sort: one relayed a diagram for mixing a Molotov cocktail; another, a question that underpins Meireles's entire oeuvre—"Which is the place of the work of art?"

Meireles created over a thousand such bottles, putting them back into circulation to change hands among millions of Brazilians. This spectacularly sly artwork continues to be a vital example of how artists can harness existing systems of value and signification to circulate marginal or dangerous ideas. Call it Meireles's message in a bottle.

Hans Haacke   *Shapolsky et al. Manhattan Real Estate Holdings, a Real-Time Social System, as of May 1, 1971* (1971)

Hans Haacke (b. 1936) is the father of politically minded conceptual art. He has long been interested in how systems work, including the cultural, financial, and political entanglements of the system in which he operates. Haacke is a pioneer among artists who query the connections between the institutions and the political and business interests of art.

Ever wonder what your New York City neighborhood looked like before Chipotle and Pinkberry moved in?

One clue is held by the infamous conceptual artwork on your left. Authored by artist-sleuth Hans Haacke, it plots out dirty real estate deals and names names—all of which set off a memorable news and public-relations furor inside and outside the New York art world in the 1970s.

Haacke's data-rich installation consists of reams of information dispassionately laid out like a legal brief. Its constituent parts are detailed by the artist like so: "One hundred forty-two photos of building facades and empty lots, with typewritten information on properties, as culled from the New York County Clerk's records, each 20 × 7 inch[es] (51 × 18 cm); two excerpts of a map of New York (Lower East Side and Harlem) with properties marked, and six charts outlining business relations within a real estate group, each 24 × 20 inch[es] (61 × 51 cm)."

If the parts appear innocuous, the project hides a stiletto in its boot. The investigation chronicles two decades of fraud committed by real estate investor Harold J. Shapolsky, one of the most notorious slumlords in New York City. Using public records, Haacke unearthed dozens of shell corporations Shapolsky and his family used to amass "the largest concentration of real estate under the control of a single group" in New York City. Other material Haacke disclosed includes the landlord's addresses, their block and lot numbers, lot sizes, and building types, as well as information on the properties' shadowy ownership, such as the names of owning corporate entities, dates of acquisitions, costs of the mortgages, assessed land values, and the names of Shapolsky's associates.

Made for inclusion in *Systems*, a solo exhibition that was due to open at the Solomon R. Guggenheim Museum in the spring of 1971, Haacke's work amounted to a searing indictment of a powerful New York City real estate family. The Shapolskys, the record shows, had important museum-going friends. A month before the scheduled opening, Guggenheim director Thomas Messer canceled the show—because the artist refused to remove this work and a related piece.

Messer explained his rationale in a candid letter to Haacke. He characterized the installation as "muckracking" and exposed the museum's vested interests to direct sunlight. "It is well understood," he wrote, "that art may have social and political *consequences* but these, we believe, are furthered by indirection and by the generalized, exemplary force that works of art may exert upon the environment, not, as you propose, by using political means to achieve political ends, no matter how desirable these may appear to be in themselves."

No dictator could have put his demand for "neutral," nonpolitical art more eloquently. By tracing real estate to its actual owners, Haacke revealed the power structures not only of slum empires but of museums too.

Philip Guston   *San Clemente*
(1975)

After Philip Guston (1913–1980) ditched abstract painting in 1968,
he embraced a vulgar, raw, and comic realism that increasingly
sought to address the world and his place in it. Often featuring
ominous Klansmen-like figures, his paintings and prints tapped
into the general cultural malaise that followed the optimism of
the 1950s and countercultural utopianism of the 1960s.

"The war, what was happening to America, the brutality of the world. What kind of man am I, sitting at home, reading magazines, going into a frustrated fury about everything—and then going into my studio to adjust a red to a blue. I thought there must be some way I could do something about it."

Philip Guston was looking back on his frustrations as an abstract painter, nearly a decade after the assassinations of Martin Luther King Jr. and Robert F. Kennedy; after Richard Nixon won the White House with merely 43 percent of the popular vote; three years after Lieutenant William Calley received a presidential pardon for killing twenty-two Vietnamese civilians; and three years after the Watergate scandal brought Nixon down.

Having turned from abstraction to figuration in 1968—setting off an art-world scandal that rivaled Bob Dylan going electric—Guston produced a suite of ink drawings and a single painting that savaged a man already considered America's most detestable president. The drawings were published posthumously as *Philip Guston's Poor Richard* (2001). The painting crystallized the repugnance and fury Guston felt for a world figure beyond redemption.

Guston painted from outrage. "One could make a list of all the negative things [that compel me to] continue painting," he declared in *Philip Guston: A Life Lived* (1982), "and [it] would include things like boredom, disgust, all the things you're not supposed to think about. It's not inspiration . . . but anger." Picasso's 1937 etching cycle *Dream and Lie of Franco* was a direct precursor; but so was Goya, who channeled both a hatred of superstition and the abuses of Enlightenment reason into prints and paintings that did their share of power-bashing.

Titled *San Clemente* after the small California town that served as Nixon's "Western White House," Guston's painting has "Tricky Dick" as the very picture of rottenness. Made one year after Nixon's resignation, it conflates two reported facts about the ex-president. The first is an infamous 1971 photo of him strolling along a beach in a stiff dark suit; the second is the news that he had developed a painful case of phlebitis, a debilitating but non-life-threatening condition that swelled his leg to twice its normal size.

The resulting picture, which is all hot pinks and shameful reds, features Nixon, with bloodshot eyes, hairy jowls, and a penis-like nose, looking over his shoulder regretfully as he drags his bandaged limb across the sands. Besides having a dick for a face, the man is all diseased leg. His bloated and veiny shank stands in for his malignant state. It bursts the confines of his sock and ratty suit much like his criminal activities poisoned the office of the president of the United States. Consider Guston's portrait of Nixon's raging degeneracy a cautionary tale of the ravages of political corruption.

Cindy Sherman (b. 1954) uses photography to conceal her own personality by taking on different identities. Together with other artists who came up in the 1980s—among them, Barbara Kruger, Robert Longo, Sherrie Levine, and Louise Lawler—Sherman continues to interpret mass-media consumerism and contemporary image culture critically. Her *Untitled Film Stills* alternately construct and deconstruct the concept of womanhood as inscribed in popular images.

In the fall of 1977, a twenty-three-year-old artist from Long Island named Cindy Sherman began an experiment. What would happen, she thought, if she put on makeup, wigs, and vintage clothing and took pictures of herself in 1950s-style fan-magazine poses? The result was a revelation in the way people read or misread images.

Before Facebook, YouTube, Instagram, and the tyranny of selfies, Sherman hit a nerve by making herself the star of her own photographs. For three years, she snapped away at herself, assuming stereotypical roles that were, at once, both uncanny and familiar. Her female characters ran the gamut: the sex kitten, the housewife, the party girl, the society lady, the damsel in distress. Thirty-six months later, she had amassed sixty-nine revealingly self-centered pictures. She only stopped, she says, when she ran out of clichés.

Sherman's photographs in *Untitled Film Stills* are like the surreal McCoy—the eight-by-ten glossies that film production companies used to promote the impostures of Tinseltown make-believe. They are also, tellingly, fictions about other fictions. Though they always feature the artist, Sherman's photographs are never really self-portraits. Instead, they are calculated deceits perpetrated with a camera to investigate truths about gender, vulnerability, identity, and power.

Take *Untitled Film Still #21*, Sherman's best-known work from the series. The artist is pictured playing the part of a small-town ingenue in her own big-city production, which draws directly from a history of television and movie images. There's the costuming from *Breakfast at Tiffany's*, the anxious look on the actress's face, the suspenseful angle of the camera. Besides condensing an entire movie into a single frame, Sherman also taps into a powerful cultural wellspring. Audiences who see this photograph recall fictions like Coke foaming from a bottle.

In Sherman's now canonical series, the artist manipulates the viewer into an encounter with the slipperiness of identity and the falsehood of feminine cliché. Though she has repeatedly rejected the idea that there are explicit narratives or social messages in her work, there is no denying the political implications of this and other images in *Untitled Film Stills*. By serially recasting her own identity as woman, Sherman demonstrates that photography—conventionally pitched as the truth-telling medium—also allows people to be someone they're not.

25

Jenny Holzer   *Truisms*
(1978–87)

A LITTLE KNOWLEDGE CAN GO A LONG WAY
A LOT OF PROFESSIONALS ARE CRACKPOTS
A MAN CAN'T KNOW WHAT IT'S LIKE TO BE A MOTHER
A NAME MEANS A LOT JUST BY ITSELF
A POSITIVE ATTITUDE MAKES ALL THE DIFFERENCE IN THE WORLD
A RELAXED MAN IS NOT NECESSARILY A BETTER MAN
A SENSE OF TIMING IS THE MARK OF GENIUS
A SINCERE EFFORT IS ALL YOU CAN ASK
A SINGLE EVENT CAN HAVE INFINITELY MANY INTERPRETATIONS
A SOLID HOME BASE BUILDS A SENSE OF SELF
A STRONG SENSE OF DUTY IMPRISONS YOU
ABSOLUTE SUBMISSION CAN BE A FORM OF FREEDOM
ABSTRACTION IS A TYPE OF DECADENCE
ABUSE OF POWER SHOULD COME AS NO SURPRISE
ACTION CAUSES MORE TROUBLE THAN THOUGHT
ALIENATION PRODUCES ECCENTRICS OR REVOLUTIONARIES
ALL THINGS ARE DELICATELY INTERCONNECTED
AMBITION IS JUST AS DANGEROUS AS COMPLACENCY
AMBIVALENCE CAN RUIN YOUR LIFE
AN ELITE IS INEVITABLE
ANGER OR HATE CAN BE A USEFUL MOTIVATING FORCE
ANIMALISM IS PERFECTLY HEALTHY
ANY SURPLUS IS IMMORAL
ANYTHING IS A LEGITIMATE AREA OF INVESTIGATION
ARTIFICIAL DESIRES ARE DESPOILING THE EARTH
AT TIMES INACTIVITY IS PREFERABLE TO MINDLESS FUNCTIONING
AT TIMES YOUR UNCONSCIOUS IS TRUER THAN YOUR CONSCIOUS MIND
AUTOMATION IS DEADLY
AWFUL PUNISHMENT AWAITS REALLY BAD PEOPLE
BAD INTENTIONS CAN YIELD GOOD RESULTS
BEING ALONE WITH YOURSELF IS INCREASINGLY UNPOPULAR
BEING HAPPY IS MORE IMPORTANT THAN ANYTHING ELSE
BEING HONEST IS NOT ALWAYS THE KINDEST WAY
BEING JUDGMENTAL IS A SIGN OF LIFE
BEING SURE OF YOURSELF MEANS YOU'RE A FOOL
BELIEVING IN REBIRTH IS THE SAME AS ADMITTING DEFEAT
BOREDOM MAKES YOU DO CRAZY THINGS
CALM IS MORE CONDUCIVE TO CREATIVITY THAN IS ANXIETY
CATEGORIZING FEAR IS CALMING
CHANGE IS VALUABLE BECAUSE IT LETS THE OPPRESSED BE TYRANTS
CHASING THE NEW IS DANGEROUS TO SOCIETY
CHILDREN ARE THE CRUELEST OF ALL
CHILDREN ARE THE HOPE OF THE FUTURE
CLASS ACTION IS A NICE IDEA WITH NO SUBSTANCE
CLASS STRUCTURE IS AS ARTIFICIAL AS PLASTIC
CONFUSING YOURSELF IS A WAY TO STAY HONEST
CRIME AGAINST PROPERTY IS RELATIVELY UNIMPORTANT
DECADENCE CAN BE AN END IN ITSELF
DECENCY IS A RELATIVE THING
DEPENDENCE CAN BE A MEAL TICKET
DESCRIPTION IS MORE VALUABLE THAN METAPHOR
DEVIANTS ARE SACRIFICED TO INCREASE GROUP SOLIDARITY
DISGUST IS THE APPROPRIATE RESPONSE TO MOST SITUATIONS
DISORGANIZATION IS A KIND OF ANESTHESIA
DON'T PLACE TOO MUCH TRUST IN EXPERTS
DON'T RUN PEOPLE'S LIVES FOR THEM
DRAMA OFTEN OBSCURES THE REAL ISSUES
DREAMING WHILE AWAKE IS A FRIGHTENING CONTRADICTION
DYING AND COMING BACK GIVES YOU CONSIDERABLE PERSPECTIVE
DYING SHOULD BE AS EASY AS FALLING OFF A LOG
EATING TOO MUCH IS CRIMINAL
ELABORATION IS A FORM OF POLLUTION
EMOTIONAL RESPONSES ARE AS VALUABLE AS INTELLECTUAL RESPONSES
ENJOY YOURSELF BECAUSE YOU CAN'T CHANGE ANYTHING ANYWAY
EVEN YOUR FAMILY CAN BETRAY YOU
EVERY ACHIEVEMENT REQUIRES A SACRIFICE
EVERYONE'S WORK IS EQUALLY IMPORTANT
EVERYTHING THAT'S INTERESTING IS NEW
EXCEPTIONAL PEOPLE DESERVE SPECIAL CONCESSIONS
EXPIRING FOR LOVE IS BEAUTIFUL BUT STUPID
EXPRESSING ANGER IS NECESSARY
EXTREME BEHAVIOR HAS ITS BASIS IN PATHOLOGICAL PSYCHOLOGY
EXTREME SELF-CONSCIOUSNESS LEADS TO PERVERSION
FAITHFULNESS IS A SOCIAL NOT A BIOLOGICAL LAW
FAKE OR REAL INDIFFERENCE IS A POWERFUL PERSONAL WEAPON
FATHERS OFTEN USE TOO MUCH FORCE
FEAR IS THE GREATEST INCAPACITATOR
FREEDOM IS A LUXURY NOT A NECESSITY
GIVING FREE REIN TO YOUR EMOTIONS IS AN HONEST WAY TO LIVE
GOING WITH THE FLOW IS SOOTHING BUT RISKY
GOOD DEEDS EVENTUALLY ARE REWARDED
GOVERNMENT IS A BURDEN ON THE PEOPLE
GRASS ROOTS AGITATION IS THE ONLY HOPE
GUILT AND SELF-LACERATION ARE INDULGENCES
HABITUAL CONTEMPT DOESN'T REFLECT A FINER SENSIBILITY
HIDING YOUR MOTIVES IS DESPICABLE

Like other artists of her generation, Jenny Holzer (b. 1950) ransacked advertising and the mass media in search of ways to make art timely. After composing nearly three hundred faux aphorisms based on clichés and commonly held truths, she successfully insinuated them into public view. Later, Holzer used electronic displays and other installation methods to fill museum galleries and animate public spaces. In 1982, she blazed *Truisms* across the jumbotron in Times Square, in New York City.

I have a sparkling memory of seeing Jenny Holzer's *Truisms* in the late 1970s in downtown Manhattan. Wheat-pasted onto a nondescript wall crammed with concert posters and personal ads, some fifty or so lines of black italic script tumbled down a sheet of oversized white paper. Read separately or apart, they resembled multiple one-line poems—or items on a deli menu, take your pick.

This daisy chain of affirmations was anonymous—"Don't place too much trust in experts," read one; "Class structure is as artificial as plastic," another—but leaned oddly on texts by a group of celebrated postmodern authors: among them, Roland Barthes, Michel Foucault, and Jean Baudrillard. The artist, it happens, had encountered their knotty linguistic theories as a fellow at the Whitney Independent Study Program. Her deadpan versions of these authors' maxims voice their frequently abstruse ideas in plain language and, more importantly, on the street itself.

Made chiefly for the public domain, Holzer's *Truisms* express multiple, even contradictory points of view. They were intended principally to evoke incomplete thoughts in complete sentences. If any consistent viewpoint emerges from their provocations, it is that truth and authority are relative and that each person should actively exercise his or her own judgment. The political implications of that prosaically democratic idea are not to be underestimated in the aftermath of Watergate, the Vietnam War, and the era's collapsing cultural and political institutions.

Eventually, Holzer's aphorisms would make their way into galleries, museums, and biennials as large LED displays and stenciled granite and marble benches (she represented the US at the 1990 Venice Biennale and won the Golden Lion). At the same time, museum shops also saw the arrival of the artist's daftly rebarbative slogans in the form of T-shirts, posters, and baseball caps.

Like the *Godfather* trilogy, Holzer's original *Truisms* proved loads better than the sequels. Her unsigned, completely ephemeral word pieces pushed art not just past authorship and representation but beyond the art world and its narrow commercial expectations. Streetwise and nearly artless, these wall-plastered printed pages were art through the eye of the needle.

26

Robert
Mapplethorpe

Man in Polyester Suit, 1980
(1980)

Memorably referred to as "the hustler with a Hasselblad," Robert
Mapplethorpe (1946–1989) was an American photographer who
relished making elegant, formally graphic images of flowers,
nudes, celebrities, and, more controversially, gay sex. A number
of these photographs are rightly remembered today as watershed
moments. Their exhibition and publication sparked debates
about what constitutes art, the kind of artworks that should be
supported by government funds, and who should have the power
to decide the answers to such questions.

"The American people . . . are disgusted with the idea of giving the taxpayers' money to artists who promote homosexuality insidiously and deliberately."

That was North Carolina Senator Jesse Helms—the paleo-conservative culture warrior once known as the Ayatollah of the South—ranting about "filthy art" on the floor of the US Senate in 1989. Among the handful of images he condemned as too obscene to be funded by taxpayers or seen in American museums was Robert Mapplethorpe's classically deadpan *Man in Polyester Suit*.

A tightly cropped picture of the torso of Milton Moore, the artist's African American lover, wearing a neatly pressed three-piece suit with his colossal penis hanging out, the photograph remains a hot-button image for various narrow-minded moralizers. Then, as now, the picture sent Bible literalists scurrying for their Leviticus. Most tellingly, *Man in Polyester Suit* is still considered too raw to be published in the pages of *The New York Times*—or, for that matter, on the cover of the auction house catalogue that advertised the print's record sale in 2015 (it sold for $478,000).

Plus ça change, plus c'est la même chose.

A picture intended to jangle the nerves and then stomp on them, Mapplethorpe's all-purpose shocker helped ignite an all-out culture war, during a period at least as contentious as our own. Made in 1980, just before the AIDS crisis exploded into the public consciousness, the photograph acquired its iconic power in 1989, the same year the artist's solo exhibition *The Perfect Moment* began its tour of seven US venues—and just months after the artist's own death from the same under-acknowledged plague.

The brouhaha over Mapplethorpe's photos began as Helms's congressional campaign heated up. Bowing to pressure, the Corcoran Gallery of Art in Washington, DC, canceled plans to host the survey. After a local artist-run organization, the nonprofit Washington Project for the Arts, stepped in to stage the exhibition, the showdown over the artist's photographs moved on to the show's next venue, Cincinnati's Contemporary Arts Center. On opening night, April 7, 1990, the center was raided by police; its director, Dennis Barrie, was indicted for "pandering obscenity." Six months later, both the center and Barrie were acquitted by a jury of eight regular Ohioans.

Ironically, Mapplethorpe didn't receive a dime of taxpayer money for his art. That mitigating fact, though, did not keep his photographs from being a target for bigots like Helms. Works like *Man in Polyester Suit* cemented the artist's gay outlaw status while asking a set of questions that remain front and center at a time of maximum factionalism in America. Should tax dollars support the arts? Who decides what is "obscene" or "offensive" in public exhibitions? If art is a form of free speech—and it has long been recognized as such in the US—is it a violation of the First Amendment to revoke federal funding on grounds of offensiveness or obscenity?

27

Joseph Beuys   *7000 Oaks*
(1982)

documenta 7   1982 Kassel   Joseph Beuys – 7000 Eichen

Joseph Beuys (1921–1986) was among the most prolific and
influential artists of the twentieth century. A sculptor, installation
artist, performer, theorist, politician, and pedagogue, he developed
an "extended definition of art" that emerged from a profound
humanism, a credulous dalliance with theosophy, and engaged
readings in social philosophy. He channeled these ideas through
prophetic actions. Just as Jeremiah used wineskins and linen
belts to impart Yahweh's message, Beuys employed felt, fat, a live
coyote, and thousands of oak trees to spread his gospel of social
betterment through art.

All art should be useful. This was the central premise behind Joseph Beuys's seminal concept of "social sculpture." With a neo-Franciscan conviction that the "social organism is a work of art" and that "everyone is an artist," the German artist evangelized art's potential to transform society with the fiery zeal of Martin Luther.

Like Francis of Assisi, Beuys believed in practicing what he preached. The father of what is today termed either "social practice" or "socially engaged art," Beuys literalized his influence in a sculpture-cum-collective-performance titled *7000 Oaks*. Launched in 1982 at the international art exhibition Documenta 7 in Kassel, Germany, Beuys's pioneering ecological art project involved planting seven thousand tree saplings, each paired with a four-foot-high basalt column, which he set down like a mini-menhir to mark the tree's growth.

At Documenta 7, Beuys first piled up the project's seven thousand stones on the lawn of Kassel's Museum Fridericianum like cordwood. Then, each time a tree was planted, the stack shrank by a single stone. Beuys potted the first tree and stone on March 16 of that year. The last pair was set down five years later, in 1987, at the opening of Documenta 8. The final works were planted by Beuys's son Wenzel, as Beuys had passed away eighteen months earlier from heart failure.

The Kassel phase of Beuys's massive reforestation project turned out to be only the beginning of a much larger campaign of environmental, urban, and artistic renewal. It proved both a symbolic representation of an ecological ideal and a working model for practical social action. Individual plantings were managed by the Free International University, which Beuys cofounded. The site proposals, crucially, were submitted and negotiated by residents, councils, schools, and other local associations throughout Germany.

As the artist put it in one of his many attempts to articulate a politics of tree planting: "I believe that planting these oaks is necessary not only in biospheric terms, that is to say, in the context of matter and ecology, but in that it will raise ecological consciousness—raise it increasingly, in the course of the years to come, because we shall never stop planting." Following Beuys's example, many more single trees with stones have since been placed at strategic sites around the world. These include plantings at the Oslo National Academy of the Arts, the Minneapolis Sculpture Garden, and at 548 West Twenty-Second Street in New York City.

In terms of art-world influence, this trailblazing work was the little acorn that has become the oak.

28

Adrian Piper   *My Calling (Card)*
                              #1 and #2
                              (1986–90)

> **Dear Friend,**
> I am black.
> I am sure you did not realize this when you made/laughed at/agreed with that racist remark. In the past, I have attempted to alert white people to my racial identity in advance. Unfortunately, this invariably causes them to react to me as pushy, manipulative, or socially inappropriate. Therefore, my policy is to assume that white people do not make these remarks, even when they believe there are no black people present, and to distribute this card when they do.
> I regret any discomfort my presence is causing you, just as I am sure you regret the discomfort your racism is causing me.

Adrian Piper (b. 1948) makes conceptual art that reckons with the structures of racial, sexual, and gendered power. A Harvard-trained philosopher, she is celebrated as an artist who focuses on subjectivity—hers, the viewer's, and that of society at large. In 2015, she was awarded the Golden Lion at the Venice Biennale. In 2018, she was given the largest exhibition to date for a living artist at New York's Museum of Modern Art.

Adrian Piper is a pioneer of conceptual art with a special line in pithy art actions that tackle micro aggressions and defuse bigoted exchanges. In 1986, for example, she designed a pair of business cards that she used through 1990 to confront everyday instances of misogyny and racism— think unsolicited come-ons at cocktail parties and comments from the in-laws at Thanksgiving dinner.

One message, which she emblazoned on white card stock, reads in part: "Dear Friend, I am not here to pick anyone up, or to be picked up. I am here alone because I want to be here, ALONE." This is the perfect rejoinder to random sexualized boorishness. It is a stinging slap across the mugs of serial sexual harassers throughout the decades.

The second message, which the artist printed on brown paper— recalling the "brown paper bag test" that certain African American organizations used to discriminate among black Americans until the late 1950s—is equally laconic and more barbed still. Its content is like a stink bomb going off at a museum opening.

Piper's card intervention is a form of discursive jujitsu. The beneficiaries of her printed gift—which the artist has made available for viewers at her exhibitions—are not merely ambushed by their own utterances. In the parlance of Hamlet, they are hoisted with their own petard. They incur kill-me-now mortification.

As a light-skinned African American woman, Piper has long chosen to identify with the social construct of blackness while exploring both the hard facts of racism and the stubborn fiction of race. *My Calling (Card) #1* and #2 turned out to be a trailblazing work of conceptual art and a troubling psychological test. Where the artist's own racially ambiguous appearance invites racist outbursts, her surgeon's scalpel of a business card shreds the kumbaya pretensions of America's post–civil rights era.

"One of the reasons for making and exhibiting a work is to induce a reaction or a change in the viewer," Piper wrote in 1970 in a short essay titled "Art as Catalysis." By this the artist meant that art can aspire to effect social change that is both objective and subjective. *My Calling (Card) #1* and #2 is a brilliant example of an artwork that accelerates critical insight by pointing out the dodgy nature of unwanted sexual advances and the dangerously thin line separating casual prejudice from blatant racism.

29

Barbara
Kruger

*Untitled (We Don't Need
Another Hero)
(1987)*

In the 1980s, Barbara Kruger (b. 1945) began using found black-and-white images from women's magazines of the 1950s and 1960s over which she collaged pithy and provocative slogans. They proved a hit with an art world hungry for responses to a decade dominated by the conservative politics of Republican presidents Ronald Reagan and George H. W. Bush. More recently, she has constructed immersive environments inside art galleries, museums, and public buildings, covering the walls, floors, and ceilings with text and images.

"Do you know why language manifests itself the way it does in my work?" Barbara Kruger once asked an interviewer. "It's because I understand short attention spans."

A one-time graphic designer and photo editor—she studied with Diane Arbus and legendary art director Marvin Israel and worked at various print publications, among them *Vogue* and *Mademoiselle*—Kruger eventually arrived, after years of struggle, at a signature style that mimics the stripped-down sales techniques of Madison Avenue.

Take this Norman Rockwell–style image of a girl admiring a boy's flexed bicep, for instance. Frame it in red to suggest socialist agitprop. Then, montage an unrelated but apposite text banner onto it—and *presto-bang-o*, you've got a perfect piece of advertising. Made to puncture the sort of clichés harbored by the short attention spans of most men and not a few women, the work spins both sexist stereotype and mass-market inattention to important advantage.

Kruger's combinations of recognizable image and text in bold oblique Futura type were originally produced at billboard scale, aiming to seize unconnected elements from popular culture and reassemble them in a way that promoted progressive politics. Put in academic terms, Kruger appropriated two popular "signifiers" for her now iconic image-and-text collage to create an entirely new "sign." The words are taken from the title of Tina Turner's theme song for the 1985 film *Mad Max Beyond Thunderdome*. Rendered in basic black and white, the new message's oversized contradictions take on the force and scale of a PR campaign designed by Ogilvy & Mather.

Kruger further blurred the boundaries between art and advertising by licensing the merchandising of this legendary word-and-image mash-up in the form of T-shirts and postcards. Other text-and-picture collages by the artist are sold as tote bags, mugs, refrigerator magnets, and beach towels. Eye-catching, lapel-grabbing, and largely uncomplicated in their imagery and messaging, this and other Kruger artworks bear a more than passing resemblance to the categorical straightforwardness of propaganda.

Constituted as interconnected but autonomous collectives to
address the HIV/AIDS epidemic in the 1980s, the groups Silence=
Death Project and ACT UP (both est. 1987) continue to organize
and exhibit around gay rights and AIDS prevention. Their
principal aim remains action rather than art—which strengthens
rather than diminishes the power of their message.

Can art that has no individual signature connect to the masses? What would it say if it could?

Before crowdsourcing, one piece of genuinely collaborative art managed to inform, inspire, and outrage millions during the 1980s and beyond.

That work—the linguistic equation "silence=death" rendered in white Gill Sans capital letters on a black background and placed beneath a pink triangle—was the product of an alliance of six New Yorkers personally affected by the HIV/AIDS epidemic. They are Avram Finkelstein, Brian Howard, Charles Kreloff, Chris Lione, Jorge Soccarás, and Oliver Johnston (who died from AIDS-related complications in 1990).

A musician, three graphic designers, and two commercial art directors, the men first met informally as part of a "consciousness-raising group" to provide support for each other as they dealt with the deaths of friends and lovers. After a year of comradeship, discussion, and planning, they arrived at an astonishing, if mostly unintended, outcome. Together, they devised an artwork that would become the recognizable trademark image for AIDS activism and political resistance worldwide.

The group's shared effort was spurred by three main concerns. First among these was a generalized sense of impotence brought on by government silence surrounding the epidemic. Second was the group's familiarity with twentieth-century political art (they studied work by the Russian constructivists, the Art Workers' Coalition, and the Guerrilla Girls). Lastly, there was the visceral need to react to the cruelty of conservative commentators—William F. Buckley Jr., for one, wrote in the pages of *The New York Times* that people with AIDS should be "tattooed in the upper forearm, to protect common-needle users, and on the buttocks, to prevent the victimization of other homosexuals."

Besides quashing the ravings of a "crypto-Nazi," as Gore Vidal referred to Buckley in a 1968 debate, the group managed a second feat of artistic and political prestidigitation with their far-reaching message. After kicking off a successful wheat-paste poster campaign throughout New York City, the group ceded their powerful visuals to the AIDS activist organization ACT UP. That organization, whose acronym stands for AIDS Coalition to Unleash Power, subsequently unleashed the graphics to the wider world in the form of protest placards, buttons, tote bags, and T-shirts (Gran Fury, a separate but affiliated group, served as ACT UP's graphic and advertising arm).

As Finkelstein put it, "An image may be authored and so, at least at that point, arguably owned." But once that particular artwork tapped into the zeitgeist, he declared, something else happened. "From that moment on, Silence=Death belonged—and it always will—to those who respond to its call."

31 Felix Gonzalez-Torres

"Untitled" (Perfect Lovers) (1987–90)

One of the most important artists of the 1980s and 1990s, Felix Gonzalez-Torres (1957–1996) closely monitored the use of his personal biography and largely avoided being photographed— to prevent celebrity from limiting the interpretation of his work. Still, his untimely death from AIDS in 1996 has magnified the impact of the artist's use of everyday objects. Known for minimalist installations and sculptures, Gonzalez-Torres used found materials, such as lightbulbs, packaged hard candy, and stacks of printed paper, as metaphors for the process of dying and regeneration while creating intimate, political meditations on private and public life.

Ticktock goes history's clock.

There is nothing scarier than time made manifest in material. In this profoundly political, intensely elegiac sculpture, two store-purchased, black-ringed clocks measure out the brutality of lives cut short, in sixty-second increments. Placed side by side so they are nearly touching, the clocks look identical but remain utterly independent—they run in sync but eventually fall out of time with each other. The process is as inevitable as it is vexing, like dancers tripping out of step or the death of a lover. It also reflects on the relationship between Felix Gonzalez-Torres and his partner, Ross Laycock, as they lived together until Laycock's passing from the global pandemic of HIV/AIDS.

A work of art whose concision recalls William Carlos Williams's haikus and the funeral blues animating W. H. Auden's "Stop All the Clocks," Gonzalez-Torres's pair of timepieces fold dime-store familiarity and aching metaphor into a single poetic gesture. Despite the somber theme—but also because the work's instructions specify that the clocks are to be restarted once they stop—there is no mistaking the artist's final message: life propels life, in imitation of the sustaining symbolism contained within Gonzalez-Torres's other minimalism-inspired, self-replenishing creations.

In an interview with curator Bob Nickas, Gonzalez-Torres admitted to the special place this work held within his oeuvre: "Time is something that scares me . . . or used to. The piece I made with the two clocks was the scariest thing I have ever done. I wanted to face it. I wanted those two clocks right in front of me, ticking."

Conceptualism has never appeared more universal or personally poetic than in this powerful artwork. A wisp of a sculpture that is often hung high on the walls of galleries and museums, it stands as a powerful monument both to the scale of human suffering attending the AIDS crisis of the 1980s and 1990s and to the idea of loss everywhere, in every age. Something gorgeous and cruel happens in this sculpture: time stands still, then moves on as if nothing happened.

Gerhard
Richter

October 18, 1977
(1988)

Gerhard Richter (b. 1932) is considered by many to be the world's
greatest living painter. His realistic gray-scale paintings make a
crucial and urgent point: to see the world in black and white is to
live within the contours of extremism.

"Human nature is not black and white," Graham Greene once wrote, "but black and grey." These words acquire special meaning when considering Gerhard Richter's painting cycle *October 18, 1977*, one of the most moving works of political art of the last half of the twentieth century.

Richter's cycle commemorates the passing of an era. Its fifteen paintings are based on press photographs of four members of the Baader-Meinhof Group, or Red Army Faction (RAF)—a West German militant group whose bombings, kidnappings, bank robberies, and assassinations kept Europe on red alert during the 1970s. It dramatizes the death of these left-wing terrorists, as well as the demise of the ideal of Marxist revolution in the West.

Richter's canvases are titled after a particular date, like George Orwell's *1984* or On Kawara's *Today* series (1966–2014). On that baleful day, October 18, 1977, the bodies of three principal RAF members, Andreas Baader, Jan-Carl Raspe, and Gudrun Ensslin, were found dead inside their cells in Stammheim Prison, in Stuttgart. (A fourth member of the group, Ulrike Meinhof, had been found hanged in her prison cell a year earlier.) Though the deaths were officially deemed suicides, there was widespread suspicion that the radicals had been murdered by the government of the Federal Republic of Germany.

Richter based his subjects' portrayals mainly on newspaper and police photographs. He rendered the documentary value of these photographs unstable: a process of painterly smudging blurred the sharp edges, as if seen through a foggy car window, and muddied their reportorial accuracy. The results reflect a wavering realism. As Richter put it, "by way of reporting," these works "contribute to an appreciation of [our time], to see it as it is."

Doubling down on his doubt about the truthfulness of images, Richter painted his subjects in gray scale (he is on the record saying that gray "is the epitome of a non-statement" and "can only notionally be real"). The series begins with a portrait painting of Ulrike Meinhof, followed by two paintings of three members of the group being arrested; three pictures of Ensslin on her way to a police lineup; a painting of Ensslin's body hanged from prison bars; an image of Baader's cell; a painting of the record player that hid Baader's gun; two images of Baader shot and bleeding out; and three head and shoulders images of Meinhof laid out dead on her cell floor. A final image, cribbed from TV footage, confirms the radicals' mass appeal—it shows three coffins being carried through a crowd during their communal funeral.

According to critic Gertrud Koch, "What characterizes these paintings is their reference to the temporality of our imaginations, the haziness of our memory, its vagueness, the sinking into amnesia, the disappearance and blurring." There is also a sense of momentous grief: anguish over the loss of life taken early but also over the epochal failure of ideology. As Richter put it in one of the many interviews he gave, "[My paintings have] to do with the everlasting human dilemma in general: to work for a revolution and fail."

Guerrilla
Girls

*Do women have to be
naked to get into the
Met. Museum?*
(1989)

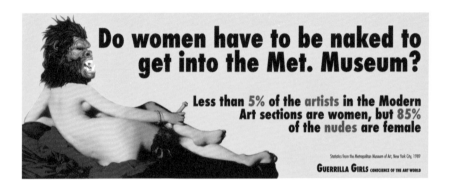

The Guerrilla Girls (est. 1985) are an anonymous group of
feminist artists devoted to fighting sexism and racism in the
art world. The collective is well known for employing culture
jamming, or "brandalism," in the form of books, posters,
billboards, presentations, and other activities. According to
the group's website, the members choose to maintain their
anonymity in order to focus on the issues, rather than the
artists' identities.

The image and language on this poster speak for themselves—or at least they ought to. Originally designed as a billboard commissioned by New York City's Public Art Fund, the advertisement was rejected on the grounds that the peacock fan brandished by the masked figure resembled a phallus. Seeing as art's officialdom felt free to monkey around with feminist satire, the art collective behind the work took charge and rented ad space on the sides of buses.

That essential act, taking representation, enfranchisement, and, ultimately, agency into the hands of female artists, has characterized the Guerrilla Girls and their activities for more than three decades. An anonymous collective whose members protect their identities by wearing gorilla masks in public and assuming heroine-inspired pseudonyms—among them, Frida Kahlo, Käthe Kollwitz, and Gertrude Stein—the Guerrilla Girls have long worked to use "facts, humor, and outrageous visuals to expose gender and ethnic bias as well as corruption in politics, art, film, and pop culture."

Dubbing themselves "the conscience of the art world," the Guerrilla Girls formed in 1985 specifically as a response to the institutional inequity on display in The Museum of Modern Art's *International Survey of Recent Painting and Sculpture*, in 1984. Of 165 artists exhibited in the survey, only 13 were women. Four years later, the group turned its attention to the permanent collection of The Metropolitan Museum of Art. Their inverted "weenie count" poured sunlight into a very dusty room: 5 percent of the artists represented in the museum's nineteenth- and twentieth-century galleries were women, while 85 percent of the nude figures were female.

To further illustrate the gender disparities that frame most things art historical, the Guerrilla Girls enlisted Jean-Auguste-Dominique Ingres's *Grande odalisque* (1814) to drive home their point. Hiding the handsome face of the odalisque—the picture of neoclassical womanliness fashioned for male enjoyment—behind their signature gorilla mask was their way of aping institutional misogyny, a force that characterizes the collecting and display habits of many museums around the world.

Since creating this iconic billboard, the Guerrilla Girls have broadened their focus and tactics to address not just gender inequality but also the lack of representation of artists of color in the art world. More recently, the group has provided crucial inspiration for the #MeToo campaign against sexual harassment.

34

David Hammons

In the Hood (1993)

David Hammons (b. 1943) has consistently outsmarted the art world, the art market, the myriad art institutions that are enamored with his work, and, ultimately, the expectations attendant on a famous African American artist. In more than fifty years of art making, he has drawn on a vocabulary of everyday symbols for prints, drawings, performances, videos, sculptures, and paintings. He once said, "Outrageously magical things happen when you mess around with a symbol."

Here's a working definition for the word "metonymy": it's what happens when you substitute the name or a part of something for the thing meant. When you mean "business executive," it's possible to say "suit." When you mean "king," you can say "the crown." When referring to a criminal, the word "hood" is often used—when it's done consistently on Fox News, it robs some 21.5 million black men of their common humanity.

Shorthand for a larger concept or complex of ideas, this rhetorical trope has its equivalent in the visual arts. The metaphorical device crops up, for example, in paintings by Ed Ruscha and René Magritte. Nowhere in my personal memory, however, has the marshaling of visual metonymy turned more meaningful or resonant than in David Hammons's sculpture-cum-installation *In the Hood*. The hood of a Champion-brand sweatshirt nailed to a wall and held open by a wire, it turns a part of a thing—a green-colored hoodie of the sort worn by countless youths—into a capacious sign that encapsulates the sorry state of race relations everywhere, but especially in the United States.

In the Hood was made nineteen years before seventeen-year-old Trayvon Martin was shot dead by George Zimmerman, a self-appointed neighborhood vigilante, who was inexplicably acquitted of murder in 2013 by a Florida court. Itself a trope for young men of color, the hoodie Hammons severed from the body of a larger sweatshirt carries associations that are centuries older than the modern racial profiling it so painfully invokes. There's Christ upon the cross, as visualized throughout centuries of Western painting and sculpture; the bloody imagery of Christian martyrdom, with its saints and sinners suffering endlessly painful mutilations and tortures, *hosanna in the highest*; and Titian's monstrous *Flaying of Marsyas* (c. 1570s), a gorgeous and cruel visual rendering of Ovid's legendary tale of injustice. A good amount of that painting's magic comes from a sense of mastery that appears nearly blithe in its concision—like Hammons's own abbreviated sculpture. If you listen carefully, a voice almost clamors from inside the open hood. It echoes Marsyas's cries as relayed by Ovid: "Help! Why are you stripping me from myself?"

Of course, a set of homegrown associations also accounts for the hoodie's rough evocativeness. The connection to the Ku Klux Klan's pointed cowls is crystal clear; so are the uneasy allusions to America's bitter history of lynching. Less familiar is the artist's penchant for installing the work in trophy fashion. When I experienced it, it was hung high, like a stuffed lion's head. *In the Hood*, a piece of industrially manufactured cloth, is an iconic artwork that was made in reaction to its own time and hauntingly anticipated demands of the future.

35

Shirin Neshat   *Women of Allah*
(1993–97)

Shirin Neshat (b. 1957) has lived much of her life outside her
native Iran, mostly in the US. Her experience of exile, of being
caught between two cultures, dominates her work. Her photos,
video installations, and films offer profound glimpses into the
complex social, religious, and political realities that shape women's
identities—hers and those of Muslim women worldwide.

Throughout history, women have been depicted in art mostly by men. This basic fact affects women everywhere, but few share the fate of exiled artist Shirin Neshat. Her photographs, videos, and short films have never been shown in Iran, her home country. More to the point, her images have been deemed so powerful that she was banned from reentering the country in 1996.

Since the early 1990s, Neshat has worked at highly contested cultural crossroads. Her images consistently straddle East and West, tradition and modernity, Islam and Christianity, the male and female gaze, beauty and violence. She has spent more than two decades making art in the face of censorship; her still and moving pictures often shoulder what the writer James Baldwin once termed "the burden of representation."

Neshat left Iran to study art in Los Angeles in 1974. A few years later, the Iranian Revolution broke out, radically changing the face and soul of her country. When Neshat returned in 1990, the brutal war between Iran and Iraq had recently ended. Islamic law dictates that women wear a chador, a veil; in the war's wake, that religious and civic obligation morphed into a badge of revolutionary pride for millions of Iranian women.

Neshat's first body of work, *Women of Allah*, dates from this period. For a series of stark black-and-white photographs, she adopted the roles of both photographer and performer, posing with various weapons while donning traditional Muslim headdress. Atop each photograph, the artist added handwritten text. In the image to your left, titled *Rebellious Silence*, the artist covers her face with verses from a poem in Farsi by Tahereh Saffarzadeh, a female writer, extolling the virtues of religious martyrdom.

A self-portrait literally split in two by the long barrel of a rifle, Neshat's haunting image invites binary readings. Among these is the very idea of arming an oppressed woman (currently in the Islamic Republic of Iran, women may be punished with up to seventy lashes or sixty days in prison for wearing "inappropriate clothing"). As Neshat said in a statement about the series, her photographs are meant to portray "willfully armed Muslim women," but the images also underscore "a far more complex and paradoxical reality behind the surface."

In *Rebellious Silence*, that paradoxical reality can be boiled down to four elements that have since become shorthand for Western representations of the Muslim world—the veil, the gun, the text, and the gaze. While these symbols have taken on an especially volatile charge since 9/11, the series *Women of Allah* expresses their universal fascination and immediacy.

Rick Lowe (b. 1961) is an artist who massively expands the
definition of his "other" job: community organizer. For more than
two decades, he has created a blueprint for creative urban renewal
that enriches lives and broadens art's precincts. *Project Row
Houses* is proof, in Lowe's words, "that life itself can also become
art, that art can be the way people live."

A change is in the air. Like cubism in the 1920s, social sculpture is currently transforming the way we think about art and society. Though the movement includes important artists such as Theaster Gates, Tania Bruguera, and SUPERFLEX, it boasts one resident Picasso: socially engaged art pioneer Rick Lowe.

Lowe is known chiefly for a single artwork, *Project Row Houses*, which stretches across five city blocks in Houston, Texas. America's longest-standing work of "social practice"—art that requires the participation of its audience to achieve social change—it is located in the Third Ward, a scrappy working-class enclave once known for its high crime rate. Today, the predominantly African American neighborhood has recovered sufficiently to attract real estate speculation—the next challenge Lowe faces in developing his art as a living community.

Project Row Houses began somewhat inauspiciously in 1993, when Lowe and a group of artist and activist friends took over two dozen derelict shotgun houses. They solicited funds and resources from, among other places, the National Endowment for the Arts, the Elizabeth Firestone Graham Foundation, and The Menil Collection, whose director gave the staff Mondays off so that they could pitch in with the renovations.

The initial idea was to mount a single art show, but the project's organic development took on a life of its own. Twenty-four years later, Lowe and his revolving company of collaborators have transformed these buildings—and some fifty others, including affordable rental units and a school—into a thriving cultural hub that offers exhibitions, artist residencies, and, most notably, housing for single mothers. Initially perplexed by the relationship between the artists and herself, one resident told Lowe: "I get it, my life is a work of art, too."

The concept of *Project Row Houses* emerged when Lowe was searching for answers to basic existential questions about becoming a political artist. "I was making painting and installation work related to political and social issues, but I was skeptical about the idea of making art about low-income people destined for wealthy individuals," he said. "One day, a student approached me and said: 'Mr. Lowe, I appreciate that your paintings and sculptures show what is happening in our community, but we don't need that. We know what happens here. If you're an artist, why can't you create a solution?'"

Lowe says this moment "turned things upside down," leading him to think about how to make art that is symbolic and poetic but which also has practical applications. He then encountered a term coined by German artist Joseph Beuys: "social sculpture." After recognizing that neighborhoods could be a medium for art, Lowe rejiggered his artistic investigations and conceived of *Project Row Houses*. An example of sustainable urban renewal—without obliterating a neighborhood's roots—*Project Row Houses* is not just the world's greatest work of social sculpture, but it is also among the most original and ambitious artworks produced anywhere in this century.

37

Kara Walker   *Gone: An Historical Romance of a Civil War as It Occurred b'tween the Dusky Thighs of One Young Negress and Her Heart* (1994)

Kara Walker (b. 1969) is among the world's most confrontational artists. She first gained international recognition for her cut-paper silhouettes in the mid-1990s. Her later work has included drawing, painting, text, shadow puppetry, film, and sculpture, all which explores past and present racial and gender stereotypes. Walker's capacious art addresses everyone—young and old, black and white, guilty-feeling and not—as ultimately sinning and sinned against.

Kara Walker shocked the world in 1994 when she affixed this narrative panorama to the walls of New York City's venerable Drawing Center. At the time, her installation went down like a double shot of discord. Seemingly out of nowhere, she turned the quaint Victorian craft of cut-paper silhouettes into a new form of history painting devoted to America's most combustible subject—race.

An astoundingly mature work for a twenty-four-year-old having her first exhibition, *Gone* proved an act of artistic recovery but also a public exorcism. The mural-sized work, which consists of clipped caricatures of antebellum figures engaged in violent and sexual acts against a white wall, actively courts controversy rather than consensus. It also conjugates an old-timey artistic practice (cut-paper portraits) with Sol LeWitt's conceptual wall painting; Walt Disney's revisionist *Song of the South* with abolitionist histories; the imagery of black minstrelsy with shitting, pissing figures locked in a chain of abjection that recalls both Goya's *Los disparates* (c. 1816–23) and Margaret Mitchell's novel *Gone with the Wind* (1936).

A perfect melding of subject and object, Walker's silhouettes—which, as she has repeatedly pointed out, function like Rorschach tests—remain to this day crystal-clear receptacles of purposefully conflicted values. An X-rated satire in a delicately decorative guise, *Gone* also proves a Trojan horse containing small devils of grinning malice. Her wall drawings of miscegenation double as abject lessons in tough love. Boiled down to an ethos, her art echoes singer-songwriter Nick Lowe: you have to be cruel to be kind.

"I wanted to make work where the viewer wouldn't walk away," Walker has said about her shadowy representations of America's dark conscience, where "he would either giggle nervously, get pulled into history, into fiction, into something totally demeaning and possibly very beautiful." That she did, in spades—and in the face of stiff opposition. In 1997, an older cohort of African American artists condemned her use of racial stereotypes and sought to organize a museum boycott of her work. To say that they failed is also to underscore how Walker's unsparing satire slew folks whom the novelist Albert Murray would likely have pegged as "the bullies of blackness."

Walker's cutouts, sculptures, films, and installations do the unspeakable: namely, inject racialized conviction into caricature. The artist's silhouettes—which she binds to stereotypes by pointing out that both speak volumes while providing little information in themselves—stack up beautifully with the best of Goya, Honoré Daumier, and Otto Dix. A perpetual effort to speak truth to power, Walker's merciless send-ups of belles and mammies, sambos and Southern gentlemen, have—in Kenneth Tynan's phrase—goaded, lacerated, and raised whirlwinds in a way that few artists (except perhaps Robert Mapplethorpe) have managed in our or any other time.

38

Chris Ofili *The Holy Virgin Mary*
(1996)

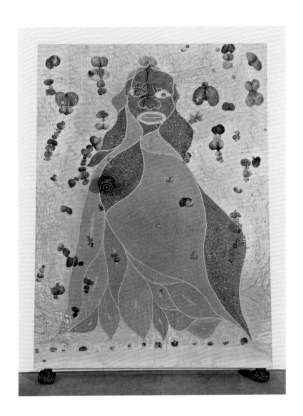

Chris Ofili (b. 1968) has helped usher Western painting into
the twenty-first century. Exuberant, kaleidoscopic, and often
politically charged, his paintings mix global influences to arrive
at rich compositions that dazzle and provoke in equal measure.
His career is proof of the idea that artists are often offered up
as canaries in the coal mines of culture.

Chris Ofili has weathered controversy and success to become one of the world's most celebrated and important artists.

In September 1999, Ofili's *The Holy Virgin Mary*—part of the exhibition *Sensation: Young British Artists from the Saatchi Collection*, on view at the Brooklyn Museum of Art (after runs at London's Royal Academy of Art and Berlin's Hamburger Bahnhof)—was scapegoated by Rudy Giuliani during his unsuccessful senatorial campaign against Hillary Clinton. Serving out his final term, the mayor, in cahoots with the conservative Catholic League, called the painting "blasphemous" and "sick stuff" and threatened to pull municipal funding unless it was removed from the show. Following legal challenges and tabloid headlines—the New York *Daily News* called the show "B'klyn Gallery of Horror"—the museum's cause prevailed.

After a pair of Manhattan gallery shows in 2007 and 2009 and a solo exhibition at The Arts Club of Chicago in 2010, Ofili held a major retrospective that opened at New York's New Museum in 2014 before traveling to the Aspen Art Museum, in Colorado. It featured new experiments with subject, materials, color, and style alongside more than lush Afrocentric pop paintings from the contentious 1990s. The most important of these, with regards to the history of First Amendment rights in the United States, is *The Holy Virgin Mary*.

Ofili's Madonna is, in the artist's words, a "hip-hop version" of the often highly sexualized renditions of the Virgin Mary on view in museums throughout the world. Large-lipped, wide-nosed, and unmistakably black, she is draped in a blue robe and stands against a gold background. The image is adorned with fluttering putti made from collaged female bottoms cut out of pornographic magazines, while clumps of elephant dung make up the Virgin's right breast (as in Renaissance depictions of the suckling mother of Christ, the robe is parted to expose a single breast); pieces of dung also serve as pedestals on which the painting stands to lean back against the wall.

Far from being irreligious, Ofili's work is an update of innumerable other depictions of women prevalent in the West, including one that predates Christianity by some twenty-eight thousand years: the voluptuous Venus of Willendorf, which was earlier this year deemed pornographic by Facebook's algorithms. Perhaps in consideration of the Later Stone Age artist who sculpted the Upper Paleolithic fertility goddess, Ofili's use of elephant dung reminds us of the earthy origins we all share—even the Holy Virgin Mary. In case anyone is still shocked, it's worth recalling Rembrandt's description of the artist as he who can find rubies and emeralds in the dung heap.

39

Francis Alÿs   *Re-enactments*
                              (2000)

After helping rebuild Mexico City following the 1985 earthquake,
the Belgian-born Francis Alÿs (b. 1959) stayed on to make art
in Mexico. More than three decades later, he is celebrated for
a brand of accessible conceptualism with a strong political bent,
increasingly so in the last decade. In 2002, he literally moved
a mountain in Peru with the help of five hundred shovel-toting
volunteers in a work called *When Faith Moves Mountains*.
In 2004's *The Green Line*, he walked the line separating the
Palestinian and Israeli zones of Jerusalem while pouring green
paint from a can.

All artworks are political, but some are more political than others. Take Francis Alÿs's videotaped action *Re-enactments*. The event belongs firmly in the annals of actions undertaken at spectacular personal risk; its politics hit home like a poem shot out of a handgun.

This work is one of Alÿs's celebrated local and international walkabout performances—including forays into Mexico City's many neighborhoods trailing a magnetic sculpture on a leash (*The Collector*, 1990–92), hardy jaunts to collect vintage snapshots of fellow strollers (*Instántaneas*, 1994–ongoing), an extended lost weekend during which the artist drifted foggily "under the influence of a different drug" for seven days (*Narcotourism*, 1996), and a nine-hour Sisyphean journey through the city center pushing a melting block of ice (*Paradox of Praxis I: Sometimes Doing Something Leads to Nothing*, 1997). The artist has described his modus operandi as follows: "What I'm interested in rarely comes through at first sight. Then, by the time I've understood what I'm looking for, I'm already on the way out of making the project."

A literal walk on the wild side, *Re-enactments* begins with Alÿs legally purchasing a 9-mm Beretta pistol at a local Mexico City gun shop. He leaves the shop with the gun firmly in his right hand and stalks the crowded city streets, a camera trailing after him. Most of the people he passes take no notice; a few scurry away or stare back. After eleven minutes of walking while toting a very visible weapon, he is stopped by police, cuffed, and roughly bundled into a police car. The artist subsequently convinced the police to re-create a full reenactment of the event, which he filmed. In galleries and museums—and on Alÿs's website, where the work is free to the public—the two versions are shown side by side as a two-channel video. The work is less a test of courage than of reality itself.

Radical and streetwise, Alÿs's performances consider not just power and the limitations imposed on individuals by civil society (to prevent outbreaks of "loner" violence, among other minor rebellions) but also the distorting effects filmed repetition has on real-life events. One obvious takeaway from *Re-enactments* is that life as lived differs markedly from life as experienced through a camera lens. Put another way, Alÿs's potentially deadly action is tamed not just by the artist's restaging but by the simple intercessional fact of its videotaping. Or as the artist says, *Re-enactments* demonstrates "how media can distort and dramatize the immediate reality of a moment."

Think of that the next time you watch CNN or binge on YouTube's Reality Channel.

Flower Thrower
(2003)

In 2010, Banksy (b. unknown) was selected by *Time* magazine for its annual list of the world's one hundred most influential people, alongside Barack Obama, Steve Jobs, and Lady Gaga. Propelled by his fame, the antiestablishment artist does brisk sales on various platforms: gift shops, galleries, and auction houses. The irony is evidently not lost on him; the artist told one interviewer, "I love the way capitalism finds a place—even for its enemies."

He's been called the Scarlet Pimpernel of the art world by the press and a vandal by fogyish authorities who fail to understand his wall drawings as popular (never mind potentially lucrative) attractions. Leaving traces in Bristol (his purported hometown), New York, Vienna, Paris, and Detroit, one of the world's most prolific political artists remains faceless—a feat akin to hiding *Charlie Hebdo* behind mirrored glasses.

Banksy has revitalized the phenomenon of street art in this century. According to author Felix Braun, the moniker is shortened from the original street tag "Robbin Banx." Moving beyond simple tagging, the use of repeated symbols or a signature to mark turf, Banksy transformed old-school graffiti into a more substantive genre: political cartooning targeting globalization and its discontents. His art involves the application of spray paint through cardboard stencils. It's sardonically figurative and antiauthoritarian. It's also instantly recognizable and readable, like a traffic sign. Not to mention, the work is perfect for the cool-hunting that characterizes our social-media age.

A hanging Klansman (Birmingham, Alabama), kissing coppers (Brighton, England), a drunk and stoned Mickey and Minnie Mouse (Los Angeles)—these are just some of the hundreds of figures with which Banksy has covered surfaces in public parks, on private buildings, and on roadway billboards in cities around the world. Arguably, his most popular intervention is the wall drawing *Flower Thrower* (of which the work on your left is a lithographic multiple). An image that breathes new life into the term *détournement*, it can be defined using the programmatic lingo of *soixante-huitard* situationists: it turns the expressions of the capitalist system and its media culture against itself.

The work, which appears on the front and back cover of Banksy's punning 2005 book, *Wall and Piece*, was first spotted on the main road from the village of Beit Sahour, near Bethlehem, in the West Bank. The stencil was lifted from a stock press photo of an anonymous protester. It depicts a male figure in black and white wearing a backward baseball cap and a bandanna over his face. Captured mid-throw, the demonstrator's stance anticipates violence—he's either a modern-day David or an unregenerate goon. The drawing's clincher: instead of a rock or a Molotov cocktail, the object he's hurling is a bouquet of colored flowers.

Flower Thrower galvanizes discordant feeling around an intractable conflict the way 1970s Herblock cartoons once did about Watergate, times a thousand. A startling image in a desert of hope, it publicly calls for Elvis Costello's trinity of peace, love, and understanding, in a place that has seen precious little of all three. Call it *existencilism*.

41   Kerry James   *Black Painting*
       Marshall   (2003–6)

For more than three decades, Kerry James Marshall (b. 1955) has
commandeered the length and breadth of Western art history and
painted it black. In a 2012 interview, the artist laid bare his artistic
approach: "It is possible to transcend what is perceived to be
the limitations of a race-conscious kind of work. It is a limitation
only if you accept someone else's foreclosure from the outside . . .
You are limited only by your ability to imagine possibilities."

Blackness—which is not a color but the absence of color—has been wielded by Kerry James Marshall as both a pigment and a rhetorical device from the beginning of his storied career. His paintings propose, with respect to the Western canon's lily whiteness, a "counter-archive" to more than six centuries of black invisibility.

Like the problem of visibility itself, Marshall's approach is both simple and highly complex. Since approximately 1980, the artist has painted every one of his figures using only three kinds of black: carbon black, originally made from soot; mars black, made from synthetic iron oxide; and ivory black, fashioned from burned animal bones.

The artist's paintings are executed using an old master's control of pigment: Marshall takes these different blacks, mixes them together, incorporates ocher, umber, and blues, to produce seven distinct versions of black. In many cases, his figures appear barely distinguishable from their backgrounds, forcing viewers into an experience of pitch-colored perception that requires more than the mere adjusting of one's eyes.

Marshall's ability to confound the legibility of his figures, while establishing a working analogy between painterly visuality and historical visibility, is nothing short of genius. While the entirety of his oeuvre has given presence to the absence of black bodies in art history's skewed visual archive, his black-on-black paintings make that proposition fundamentally radical. Think Ralph Ellison's *Invisible Man* meets Ad Reinhardt's "last paintings" crossed with Malcolm X's speech "The Ballot or the Bullet."

A genuine tour de force, *Black Painting* presents, as its title suggests, an African American narrative that portrays the moment before the December 4, 1969, murder of Fred Hampton, the chairman of the Illinois chapter of the Black Panther Party, at the hands of Chicago police. The picture features—among other hard-to-see details—a jet-black bedroom, a Black Panther flag, a copy of Angela Davis's jailhouse book *If They Come in the Morning: Voices of Resistance*, and the bodies of Hampton and his fiancée, Akua Njeri.

Hampton is depicted sleeping. Njeri, a fellow militant, is propped up in bed, listening intently, it seems, for a cue that will signal the final chapter of her and her partner's shocking story. The picture not only conflates literal and symbolic aspects of blackness; it also combines radical aesthetics, revolutionary politics, and a lights-out narrative worthy of history's most tragic episodes.

"Extreme blackness plus grace equals power," Marshall has said by way of formulating an eloquent artist's statement. "It's a kind of stereotyping, but my figures are never laughable." In point of fact, Marshall's use of stereotype in *Black Painting* is so laugh-proof it dares you to take it lightly. This canvas, above all others made this century, takes racist clichés and transforms them into their opposite. This is history painting that dramatizes a fundamental fact: where race and power relations are concerned, history is hard to see.

Paul Chan   *Waiting for Godot in New Orleans*
(2007)

Paul Chan (b. 1973) is an artist who has, despite personal
statements to the contrary, pushed to unite the fields of art and
social activism. In 2002, Chan was part of Voices in the Wilderness,
an American aid group that broke US sanctions by working in
Baghdad prior to the US invasion. In 2004, he produced *The
People's Guide to the Republican National Convention*, a free map
distributed to help protesters maneuver through New York City
during the Republican National Convention.

The first time that Paul Chan visited New Orleans in 2006, a year after Hurricane Katrina flooded 80 percent of the city, the artist was struck by the eerie quiet that haunted neighborhoods like Gentilly and the Lower Ninth Ward. Wherever he paused to survey the streets, silence followed— no traffic sounds, no pedestrians to-ing and fro-ing on the sidewalks, no construction crews busying themselves with restoration and repairs.

Chan's response to the silent city was to imagine an outdoor performance that could match the Big Easy's newfound desolation. Samuel Beckett's laconic play *Waiting for Godot*, in which "nothing happens, twice," came to mind. A production of Beckett's theater piece had famously enabled Susan Sontag to express the suffering and resilience of a tragically postponed population—the residents of war-torn Sarajevo in 1993.

Chan won the support of local artists, educators, and community leaders, as well as that of the New York–based arts-commissioning organization Creative Time and the actor Wendell Pierce, a New Orleans native, known for his roles in the cable series *The Wire* and *Treme*. The artist and his crew put on four performances of Beckett's play at Hurricane Katrina's ground zero: two were staged in the middle of an intersection in the Lower Ninth Ward, and another two in the front yard of an abandoned house in Gentilly.

Beckett's play served as a potent metaphor for the city's destruction and being forgotten. "Seeing *Godot* embedded in the very fabric of the landscape of New Orleans was my way of re-imagining the empty roads, the debris, and, above all, the bleak silence as more than the expression of mere collapse," Chan said. "There is a terrible symmetry between the reality of New Orleans post-Katrina and the essence of this play, which expresses in stark eloquence the cruel and funny things people do while they wait: for help, for food, for hope."

As important as the final performances of Godot were in drawing attention to New Orleans, Chan's mobilization of the city's residents was even more so. That bigger social production involved, among other elements, free art seminars, potluck dinners, educational programs, theater workshops, meetings with numerous local groups, the publication of a book that channeled multiple voices, and an overall commitment on the part of everyone involved to jointly author, come hell or more high water, Beckett's powerful tragicomedy. Additionally, a "shadow" fund was established for rebuilding efforts in the neighborhoods where the play was presented.

The greater purpose of Chan's *Godot* wasn't merely to make newspaper headlines or encourage more disaster tourism in New Orleans. Instead, the idea was to put into practice a fundamental principle of socially engaged art many artists fail to grasp, despite hundreds of thousands of well-meaning grant proposals. That is, simply, that a truly transparent, genuinely collaborative arts project fundamentally needs community authorship to succeed. Failing that, to quote *Waiting for Godot*: "Nothing happens. Nobody comes, nobody goes. It's awful."

43   Shepard
Fairey
(after Mannie
Garcia)

Barack Obama "HOPE"
(2008)

In the words of the critic Peter Schjeldahl, Shepard Fairey
(b. 1970) has the distinction of having created "the most
efficacious American political illustration since *Uncle Sam
Wants You.*" Rather than rest on his laurels, the artist has
greeted Donald Trump's authoritarian presidency with activist
art created for such movements as Black Lives Matter and
the Women's March.

A "streamlined, iconic image" was what Los Angeles–based graphic artist Shepard Fairey had in mind for Barack Obama's 2008 presidential campaign. He took his cue to design a picture of the candidate two weeks ahead of Super Tuesday—the date when a whopping twenty-four states and American Samoa hold primary elections and caucuses to select the Democratic and Republican candidates for president of the United States.

Hillary Clinton was ahead in the polls. Fairey's challenge was, therefore, mammoth: to design an emblem that would help Obama win the Super Bowl of politics. Not only did the artist have to come up with a transformational portrait in less than a fortnight; he also had to design an image that would channel the candidate's progressive intellectual appeal into the viral visual equivalent of DJ Khaled's "All I Do Is Win."

Fairey has acknowledged—shockingly—that he worked to "de-racialize" Obama by using a patriotic "red, white, and blue color palette." (This and other observations about the poster on your left emerged in a 2012 *Harvard Journal of Law and Technology* article regarding the artist's subsequent copyright dispute with the Associated Press.) It seems that representing a presidential candidate as a patriot and a black man in twenty-first-century America was judged to be impossible.

The artist's next challenge was to represent the man who would become the nation's first African American commander in chief in an image that rendered his distinct person instantly "familiar, American, and presidential." Fairey turned to a well-worn civic likeness. The template he used was a dreamy photograph of John F. Kennedy in three-quarter view—an image which, in turn, became a US Postal Service commemorative stamp in 2017.

Though it was never officially adopted by the Obama campaign (because of the very copyright issues that beset the image), Fairey's *Hope* poster exploded the idea of political virality the way Russian hackers and bots have done for fake news. The artist's initial print run of seven hundred posters soon became ten thousand. These, in turn, self-reproduced like spores through free downloads; Obama's image was replicated for countless electoral events and millions of Facebook pages. Fairey masterminded the first full-blown internet meme in the history of presidential politics.

In the first version of Fairey's poster, the text below the blue-and-red stars-and-stripes image of Obama read "progress." After some back and forth with the campaign—Democratic consultants were apparently convinced that conservatives equate the terms "progressive" and "socialist"—that word was changed to "hope," to better connect with the candidate's message.

Both a recognizable portrait of the man who became POTUS forty-four, against the run of America's racist history, and an emblem that transcends the representational limitations of a photograph, *Hope* hangs in the National Portrait Gallery, in Washington, DC. It packs several contradictions— among them, genuine idealism and realpolitik—into a single image.

The son of a banished revolutionary poet, Ai Weiwei (b. 1957)
grew up under the harsh conditions of internal exile. In 1981, he
moved to the US, where he would stay for more than a decade.
Only later, back in Beijing, after years of activism as a publisher,
curator, architect, artist, and social commentator, would he come
into contact with the Chinese authorities. For criticizing the
government's rampant corruption and the country's lack of human
rights, he has been beaten, jailed, and effectively exiled to the
West. Ai's use of social media, including Twitter and Instagram,
remains among his chief weapons.

There are instances in history when artists have confronted political power directly. In our time, only one has taken on a global superpower and succeeded in exposing its corrupt rule: the Chinese polymath Ai Weiwei.

Filmmaker, photographer, designer, architect, activist, blogger, dissident—these are just a few of the roles inhabited by the world's most famous artist. A figure with a boldface name and an instantly recognizable shaggy mug, Ai has used his pop-star status to advocate for political and social change. In the process, he has obliterated the line between art and activism—in ways few contemporary artists have before him.

Ai's global activism began in earnest when he shone a klieg light on a local disaster that the Chinese government partly caused, covered up, then tried to make disappear. In 2008, a 7.9 magnitude earthquake struck Sichuan, collapsing thousands of schoolrooms throughout the province. Parents fingered unscrupulous officials for the shoddy construction that resulted in the deaths of thousands of children. Others blamed China's central government. A campaign to silence families, ahead of the upcoming Beijing Olympics, was exposed.

Working with a team of volunteers to gather the names of the victims, Ai published information about 5,219 missing children on his blog—Chinese authorities took the webpage down faster than a Mao sex tape. On a visit to Chengdu, Sichuan's capital, Ai was detained by the police at his hotel. He had traveled to testify on behalf of an activist on trial on charges of "subversion of state power," but he was beaten and prevented from going to court. The injuries he suffered proved life-threatening: in Munich, where he was preparing a major exhibition at the city's iconic Haus der Kunst, he suffered a brain hemorrhage.

Besides documenting his attack and injuries on the internet—along with his CAT scan—Ai channeled the moral force of his "Sichuan Earthquake Citizens' Investigation" into a 330-foot mural for the facade of Haus der Kunst, which was once Hitler's favorite art museum (it was inaugurated in 1937 to celebrate the Fuhrer's *Great German Art Exhibition*). Titled *Remembering*, the artist's massive composite portrait of injustice and loss was constructed from nine thousand colored school satchels. Together, they spelled out a phrase in Chinese, borrowed from a grieving mother: "She lived happily for seven years in this world."

Ai also spelled out his rejection of China's one-party system in a 2008 blog post: "This is a society without citizens. A person with no true rights cannot have a complete sense of morality or humanity. In a society like this, what kind of responsibility or duty can an individual shoulder? What kinds of interpretations and understandings of life and death will he have?"

Tania
Bruguera

Tatlin's Whisper #6
(Havana Version)
(2009/2014)

Tania Bruguera (b. 1968) has used performance, installations, and pedagogy to create art that reaches for solutions to real-world problems, such as immigrants' rights and the global wealth gap. "A well-made painting or sculpture doesn't do much to improve economic or political inequality," she says. "What I'm proposing is a model for activist art, an art that can see beyond what exists today in society and imagine possible futures."

Cuban installation and performance artist Tania Bruguera has declared: "Useful art is the art of the 21st century. It's art made by citizens and for citizens. It's not art that is interested in improving the system; it's art that wants to destabilize things in order to change the system."

A seismic force in today's international art world, Bruguera has captured the attention of a nation with a single artwork. Her conscience-driven, activist art demands its own label, which she has called "artivism."

In 2009, Bruguera enacted one of the world's best-known pieces of performance art. Conducted within the framework of the Tenth Havana Biennial, the work consisted of a microphone, a podium, two loudspeakers, and what the artist termed "one minute free of censorship per speaker." Bruguera titled the work *Tatlin's Whisper #6 (Havana Version)* in homage to Vladimir Tatlin's unrealized utopian *Monument to the Third International*. In the fall of 2014, the artist revisited the performance in a video installation at New York's Guggenheim Museum as part of an exhibition of contemporary art from Latin America.

On December 30, 2014—less than two weeks after President Barack Obama announced that the United States would normalize relations with Cuba—Bruguera attempted to reenact the work in Havana's Revolution Square. The square is dominated by a 358-foot tower memorializing Cuba's nineteenth-century independence leader José Martí, a mural of Che Guevara, and the closely guarded offices of Cuba's then president, Raúl Castro. Bruguera was arrested along with fifty other dissidents and opposition figures. Her computer, cell phone, and passport were confiscated; she was denied legal representation; and, in contravention of Cuban law, she was held in legal limbo for nine months.

Bruguera fought back. She rallied friends and colleagues, called news conferences, staged readings of Hannah Arendt's *The Origins of Totalitarianism*, and embarked on a social-media campaign. The importance of Bruguera's performance grew in direct proportion to the arbitrariness of her arrest, and global support poured in. Even in one of the least connected countries in the world—only 5 percent of Cuban households have internet access as of 2016—her message of civic optimism, creativity, and freedom of expression leapfrogged Cuba's surveillance systems and went viral.

Bruguera is pragmatic about the impact of *Tatlin's Whisper #6 (Havana Version)* on human rights in Cuba: "The government did the work for me," she told one reporter. "They changed the meaning of the work, giving a lesson in intolerance." Her performance crystallized the contradictions of a totalitarian regime and demonstrated that art can sometimes serve as a righteous bullhorn in the demand for free speech.

Christ the Saviour Cathedral Performance (2012)

Like the Chinese artist Ai Weiwei and the Cuban conceptualist Tania Bruguera, the art collective Pussy Riot (est. 2011) has thumbed its nose at the coercive power of the modern nation-state. Recently, the group has suggested that American artists follow their example. "Political art is simply essential for life in the United States right now," one member said. "It's not just about Trump. It's about Nazi groups that are calling for people to be judged according to racial characteristics and so on . . . You shouldn't be scared, you need to act."

It's been called "The Prank Heard 'Round the World."

On February 21, 2012, a group of young women in candy-colored minidresses and hand-scissored balaclavas mounted the altar of Moscow's Christ the Saviour Cathedral to perform an impassioned song.

Not exactly *Nearer My God to Thee*, what they belted out instead was an obscenity-laced "punk prayer." Titled *Holy Shit*, it went, in part: "Holy Mother, Blessed Virgin, chase Putin out!" A condemnation of the Russian Orthodox Church's unwavering support for Vladimir Putin—issued on the eve of the country's presidential elections—the ditty, intoned by the then anonymous feminist art collective Pussy Riot, provided a rallying cry for millions of Russians and non-Russians opposed to the country's crypto-totalitarian regime.

Pussy Riot's performance lasted exactly forty seconds before three of the group's members—Maria Alyokhina, Yekaterina Samutsevich, and Nadezhda Tolokonnikova—were arrested and taken into custody. Held without bail, they were convicted and sentenced to two years in prison for "hooliganism" and "religious hatred" in proceedings reminiscent of Joseph Stalin's show trials. All three were set free a year later, but not before Putin and his cronies were fully revealed to be something other than advertised at the G8 summit: a ruthless gang of kleptocrats with a poisonous disregard for human rights.

The story of Pussy Riot boasts an irresistible Hollywood storyline: three charismatic (and photogenic) protagonists stand up to an oppressive dictator, evil prosecutors, and kangaroo courts, until they are released thanks to an outpouring of support by Western governments—among them, the US, France, and Germany—and celebrities such as Bono, Sting, and Madonna. Improbable as that narrative is, though, it pales in comparison to the group's real-life appeal. Among the first practitioners of performance as popular global protest, Pussy Riot literally converted the world into fans of dissident art.

Pussy Riot's years-long work of performance art—as enacted by their unwavering ethics, personal bravery, and gazillions of YouTube hits—turned a once obscure protest into a global allegory of oppression overnight. It also turned its known members, Alyokhina, Samutsevich, and Tolokonnikova, into worldwide celebrities. Today, these women are ambassadors of free speech, human rights, and activism of the noninstrumental kind. Lacing their earnest demands about voting rights and political prisoners, their pop-star fame, fickle and self-insulating as it ever is, proves both their calling card and their handicap.

Thomas Hirschhorn   *Gramsci Monument* (2013)

Thomas Hirschhorn (b. 1957) continues to create art for a nonspecialist, participative public. His series of monuments to great philosophers, while physically ephemeral, are intended to live on in the collective memory of those who experience them. The other three monuments in the series were named after the philosophers Baruch Spinoza (1999), Gilles Deleuze (2000), and Georges Bataille (2002).

A fundamental question hangs over Thomas Hirschhorn's *Gramsci Monument*. Can art—including all the objects, events, and interventions considered in this book—actually change the world?

A participatory work of art built in the form of a temporary structure, or "monument" in the Swiss artist's parlance, *Gramsci Monument* attempts the improbable: to create a living work of art in the form of a community center inside a New York City housing project. The sculpture-cum-performance was temporarily sited at the Forest Houses in the South Bronx from July 1 to September 15, 2013.

Constructed in collaboration with the New York City Housing Authority and the Dia Art Foundation (Dia's first public commission in New York since extending Joseph Beuys's tree-planting installation *7000 Oaks* to Manhattan in 1996), the project brought a series of amenities, opportunities, and aesthetic challenges to the one-time digs of rappers Fat Joe and the Diggin' in the Crates Crew.

Providing a provisional home for a daily newspaper, a computer room, a lounge, a performance stage, an exhibition space, a radio station, and space for a philosopher-in-residence (Marcus Steinweg, who studies the intersection of philosophy and art), the communal artwork also generated employment for Forest Houses residents—those who built and staffed the monument were paid at nearly double the minimum wage.

Gramsci Monument was inspired by a founder of the Italian Communist Party, the philosopher Antonio Gramsci. Gramsci spent eleven years in Benito Mussolini's prisons devising a radically egalitarian concept of working-class revolution, in which "everyone is a philosopher, though in his own way and unconsciously."

To aspire to Gramsci's ideal, though, required more than just nails, plywood, cardboard, and packing tape (the last two are signature materials for Hirschhorn). That is, the monument depended less on a physical framework than on the immersive participation of Forest Houses residents. The resulting sense of shared authorship was best expressed by one of Hirschhorn's main "partners," Erik Farmer, the president of the Resident Association of Forest Houses. "There's nothing cultural here at all," Farmer told *The New York Times*, referring to life in the South Bronx housing complex. "It's like we're in a box here, in this neighborhood . . . This is kind of like the world coming to us for a little while."

The art industry devoted thousands of column inches to pro and contra positions on the monument before, during, and after the close of the project, but Hirschhorn's work should be judged by something other than a collection of critical reviews. According to the artist, he and his collaborators proposed a new kind of provisional but pragmatic civic monument at Forest Houses.

When announcing their 2017 commission for Turbine Hall, Tate
Modern defined SUPERFLEX (est. 1993) as artists "best known
for their interests in unifying urban spaces and commenting on
society with authenticity through art." Their projects largely
propose solutions to real problems: among them, developing
alternative fuel sources, designing viable food-distribution systems,
and rigging the art market to funnel humanitarian aid to conflict
zones. The group's ongoing reconsideration of Marcel Duchamp's
antique tool, the readymade, suggests the possibility of an emerging
and increasingly practical conceptual paradigm for a new century.

Can something be both a functional object and an artwork at the same time? That is the question the members of the Danish art collective SUPERFLEX (Jakob Fenger, Rasmus Nielsen, and Bjørnstjerne Christiansen) have been asking since the group's founding in 1993. A band of visionary artists that routinely refers to its objects and activities as "tools," they also define their efforts independently of medium, as "a model or proposal that can actively be used and further utilized and modified by the user."

According to SUPERFLEX, the notion of the "readymade" has undergone fundamental changes since Marcel Duchamp coined it in 1915 to describe functional objects elevated to the status of art by simple designation. One of those changes is the complete acceptance of Duchamp's critical-conceptual method by the global art market. Another is the relatively recent rescue of conceptualism's antiestablishment edge by a small but crucial coterie of politically minded international artists.

Enter SUPERFLEX's depth charge of an artwork: *Hospital Equipment*. A gleaming tableau of surgical lamps, an instrument stand, and an operating table, the work was first assembled for an exhibition at Copenhagen's Den Frie Centre of Contemporary Art. Subsequently, the work was bought by a group of collectors, who, in keeping with a contract established with the artists, shipped it to a crucial third party. That third party was an emergency clinic in Gaza, the Al-Shifa Hospital—the medical complex that treated the largest number of wounded during the 2016 to 2017 clashes between Israelis and Palestinians.

As a ready-made artwork and a set of actual lifesaving devices, *Hospital Equipment* exhibits the qualities of a Swiss Army knife. When exhibited in a gallery or museum, it constitutes a rarefied spectator experience—albeit one with an ulterior humanitarian motive. Placed inside a working hospital, it saves lives while continuing to express an act of collective reflection that enhances the equipment's medical mission.

More than a hundred years ago, Duchamp declared that he endorsed "ideas," not "visual products." Today, SUPERFLEX proposes that those ideas can become useful products, not urinals giddily celebrated on gallery pedestals.

Charlie Hebdo (est. 1970) defines itself as secular, skeptical, atheist, far left-wing, anti-racist, and also "a punch in the face." Its "survival issue" sold nearly eight million copies. Luz, the publication's most prominent cartoonist, left the magazine in September 2015. He confessed to being "exhausted by a thousand things, mourning, pain, rage" but also "regular media coverage."

On the morning of January 7, 2015, two French Algerian brothers forced their way into the Paris offices of the French satirical weekly *Charlie Hebdo* and killed eight members of the editorial staff, a building maintenance worker, a visitor, and two policemen. Among the motives for the attack was the weekly's publication in 2011 of a cartoon of the Prophet Muhammad with the caption "100 lashes of the whip if you don't die laughing."

Following the murders, thousands of people took to the streets of Paris to express grief for the victims and support for the equal-opportunity blasphemy that has propelled France's most irreverent magazine for four decades (the journal's mission statement declares it is against false idols such as God, Wall Street, and "two cars and three cell phones"). This message of solidarity spread quickly via social media, with the slogan *Je suis Charlie*, which turned into chants, placards, and T-shirts.

Days after the massacre, the publication's remaining team of sixteen journalists hunkered down in the offices of the French daily *Libération*, on computers provided by *Le Monde*, to put together issue 1178 of *Charlie Hebdo*, known as "the survival issue." The edition, published on January 14, includes sixteen pages of new cartoons, plus previously published articles by two slain journalists and drawings by four of the publication's fallen artists.

Most memorably, the magazine's anguished, take-no-prisoners cover depicts a cartoon of the Prophet Muhammad with the headline "Tout est pardonné" (everything is forgiven). Against a solid green background— the color of paradise—the prophet wears Islam's white garments of mourning and sheds a tear while looking at the viewer. He is sketched loosely, in the style of Matt Groening or Charles Schulz, a *Charlie Hebdo* inspiration, and holds a sign that reads JE SUIS CHARLIE.

Besides reclaiming Muhammad from the terrorists, the magazine's rendering of the comically disconsolate prophet satirizes the infantile desire of fundamentalists to murder satire itself. It also casts back to a long-standing tradition of French social criticism that includes, among other honorable confrontations between freedom and censorship, the tangle between Honoré Daumier and King Louis-Philippe (Daumier was sentenced to six months in jail for depicting the king as a Gargantua). The cover of the survival issue celebrates the right to mock and blaspheme and hold nothing sacred. As a caricature, the drawing hilariously sends up death; as an exercise in free speech, it recalls the words of Medgar Evers: "You can kill a man, but you can't kill an idea."

The best cartoons are those which straddle the divide between reflection and provocation. With this issue's cover, drawn by Rénald Luzier, known as Luz, the world was gifted a rare treasure: a work of art that wrings humor from its own tragedy.

Theaster
Gates

Stony Island Arts Bank
(2015–ongoing)

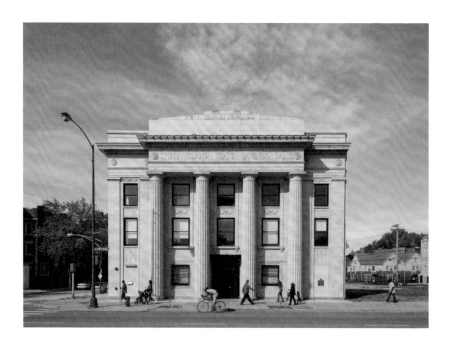

Theaster Gates (b. 1973) has trained as a gospel singer, a potter, and an urban planner, but he may be best described as "a real-estate artist." Like a Keynesian capitalist with a redistributive mission, Gates has learned how to revitalize cultural communities by using—with a nod to the cultural critic Shannon Jackson—money as material.

"No people come into possession of a culture without having paid a heavy price for it," James Baldwin once wrote. For more than a decade, Chicago-based artist, urban planner, and activist Theaster Gates has stopped just shy of raising actual cathedrals from this sentiment.

Starting with his 2006 purchase of a vacant home on East Sixty-Ninth Street and South Dorchester Avenue, Gates has been steadily rebuilding Chicago's legendary South Side. His nonprofit, the Rebuild Foundation, uses culturally driven projects as a catalyst for redevelopment, converting abandoned buildings for living and cultural use, and investing in a forgotten African American workforce.

Like many visionary developers' initiatives, Gates's urban restoration scheme—as well as other programs he has launched in cities such as Gary, Indiana; Kassel, Germany; and Detroit—pulls together private and public partners to tackle various projects. Of these, his most collaborative and ambitious is the renovation of the Stony Island Trust and Savings Bank, a vast ninety-five-year-old, 17,000-square-foot ruin. In 2013, Chicago mayor Rahm Emanuel sold the structure to an LLC controlled by Gates for one dollar. To finance the building's planned 4.5 million dollar restoration, the artist called in favors, leveraged relationships, and raised more than 1.1 million dollars from a benefit gala. Gates also sold *Bank Bonds*—artworks made from marble slabs cut from the bank itself—for five thousand dollars each. Inscribed on the *Bank Bonds* are the words "In ART We Trust."

Today, the bank's Doric columns and soaring ceilings shelter exhibitions, lectures, film screenings, a café, and various collections that the artist has reclaimed from the dustbin of history. These include the record collection of DJ Frankie Knuckles, the godfather of house music; the magazine and book collection of John H. Johnson, the founder of *Ebony* and *Jet* magazines; slides from the digitized collections of the Art Institute of Chicago and the University of Chicago; the Edward J. Williams collection of "negrobilia," racist tchotchkes that Williams initially amassed with the purpose of removing them from circulation; and, most poignantly, the gazebo where twelve-year-old Tamir Rice was shot dead in 2014 by Cleveland police for playing with a BB gun.

What Gates has achieved with *Stony Island Arts Bank* doesn't just tilt at symbolism; it creates a physical footprint for culture in an urban area haunted by the Great Migration, the postwar decline of Chicago's industrial base, and the city's current crisis around gun violence. Possessing an entrepreneur's moxie, Gates has achieved what few thought possible— he has combined the business of real estate, the activism of Rosa Parks, and what Andy Warhol once called, in a far less cynical age, "business art."

List of works

1 Francisco de Goya y Lucientes
Grande hazaña! Con muertos! (A Heroic Feat! With Dead Men!), plate 39 from *Los desastres de la guerra (The Disasters of War)*, 1810–20 (printed 1863)
Etching and aquatint
6 1/8 × 8 1/16 inches
15.5 × 20.5 cm
Yale University Art Gallery, New Haven, Connecticut. Gift of Lois Severini and Enrique Foster Gittes, BA, 1961
Photo courtesy Yale University Art Gallery

2 Eugène Delacroix
July 28: Liberty Leading the People, 1830
Oil on canvas
102 3/8 × 128 inches
260 × 325 cm
Musée du Louvre, Paris
Photo © Musée du Louvre, Dist. RMN-Grand Palais/Philippe Fuzeau/Art Resource, NY

3 J. M. W. Turner
Slave Ship (Slavers Throwing Overboard the Dead and Dying, Typhoon Coming On), 1840
Oil on canvas
35 3/4 × 48 1/4 inches
90.8 × 122.6 cm
Museum of Fine Arts, Boston. Henry Lillie Pierce Fund
Photo © 2018 Museum of Fine Arts, Boston

4 Gustave Courbet
The Stone Breakers, 1849
(destroyed 1945)
Oil on canvas
62 9/16 × 102 inches
159 × 259 cm
Formerly Galerie Neue Meister, Dresden
Photo © Staatliche Kunstsammlungen Dresden/Bridgeman Images

5 Honoré Daumier
The Third-Class Carriage, c. 1862–64
Oil on canvas
25 3/4 × 35 1/2 inches
65.4 × 90.2 cm
The Metropolitan Museum of Art, New York. H. O. Havemeyer Collection, Bequest of Mrs. H. O. Havemeyer, 1929
Photo courtesy The Metropolitan Museum of Art, New York

6 Édouard Manet
The Execution of Emperor Maximilian, 1868–69
Oil on canvas
99 3/16 × 118 7/8 inches
252 × 302 cm
Kunsthalle Mannheim, Mannheim, Germany
Photo by Cem Yücetas, courtesy Kunsthalle Mannheim

7 Käthe Kollwitz
Memorial Sheet for Karl Liebknecht, 1920
Woodcut on paper
15 7/8 × 21 15/16 inches
40.4 × 55.7 cm
Sterling and Francine Clark Art Institute, Williamstown, Massachusetts
Photo courtesy Sterling and Francine Clark Art Institute, Williamstown, Massachusetts/ Bridgeman Images

8 Vladimir Tatlin
Model of the Monument to the Third International, 1920
Photograph of wooden model
Dimensions of model: 165 3/8 × 118 1/8 × 118 1/8 inches | 420 × 300 × 300 cm
The Museum of Modern Art, New York
Digital image © The Museum of Modern Art/ Licensed by SCALA/Art Resource, NY

9   George Grosz
Plate 68 from *Ecce Homo*, 1922–23
(reproduced drawings and watercolors executed 1915–22)
Illustrated book with 100 offset lithographs
Printed by Dr. Selle & Co. A.G., Berlin
Published by Malik-Verlag, Berlin
This page: 13 11/16 × 9 13/16 inches
34.8 × 25 cm
The Museum of Modern Art, New York. The Louis E. Stern Collection
Digital image © The Museum of Modern Art/Licensed by SCALA/Art Resource, NY
Art © Estate of George Grosz/Licensed by VAGA, New York, NY

10   Max Beckmann
Departure, 1932–35
Oil on canvas, three panels
Side panels: 84 3/4 × 39 1/4 inches | 215.3 × 99.7 cm; center panel: 84 3/4 × 45 3/8 inches | 215.3 × 115.2 cm
The Museum of Modern Art, New York
Digital image © The Museum of Modern Art/Licensed by SCALA/Art Resource, NY
Art © 2018 Artists Rights Society (ARS), New York/VG Bild-Kunst, Bonn

11   Walker Evans
Bud Fields and His Family, Hale County, Alabama, 1936
Gelatin silver print
7 5/8 × 9 9/16 inches
19.4 × 24.3 cm
The J. Paul Getty Museum, Los Angeles
Digital image courtesy the Getty's Open Content Program

12   Pablo Picasso
Guernica, 1937
Oil on canvas
137 1/2 × 305 3/4 inches
349.3 × 776.6 cm
Museo Nacional Centro de Arte Reina Sofía, Madrid
Photo courtesy Museo Nacional Centro de Arte Reina Sofía, Madrid/Bridgeman Images
Art © 2018 Estate of Pablo Picasso/Artists Rights Society (ARS), New York

13   José Clemente Orozco
The Carnival of Ideologies, 1937–39
Fresco
Governor's Palace, Guadalajara, Mexico
Dimensions variable
Photo courtesy Schalkwijk/Art Resource, NY
Art © 2018 Artists Rights Society (ARS), New York/SOMAAP, Mexico City

14   Jacob Lawrence
And the migrants kept coming, panel 60 from *The Migration Series*, 1940–41
Tempera on gesso on composition board
12 × 18 inches
30.5 × 45.7 cm
The Museum of Modern Art, New York. Gift of Mrs. David M. Levy
Digital image © The Museum of Modern Art/Licensed by SCALA/Art Resource, NY
Art © 2018 The Jacob and Gwendolyn Knight Lawrence Foundation, Seattle/Artists Rights Society (ARS), New York

15   Robert Motherwell
Elegy to the Spanish Republic No. 70, 1961
Oil on canvas
69 × 114 inches
175.3 × 289.6 cm
The Metropolitan Museum of Art, New York. Anonymous Gift, 1965
Photo © The Metropolitan Museum of Art/Art Resource, NY
Art © Dedalus Foundation/Licensed by VAGA, New York, NY

16 Robert Rauschenberg
Retroactive I, 1963
Oil and silk screen on
canvas
84 × 60 inches
213.4 × 152.4 cm
Wadsworth Atheneum
Museum of Art, Hartford,
Connecticut. Gift of
Susan Morse Hilles, 1964
Photo by Allen Phillips,
courtesy Wadsworth
Antheneum
Art © Robert
Rauschenberg
Foundation/Licensed by
VAGA, New York, NY

17 Andy Warhol
Orange Disaster #5, 1963
Acrylic and silk-screen
enamel on canvas
106 × 81 1/2 inches
269.2 × 207 cm
The Solomon R.
Guggenheim Museum,
New York. Gift of Harry
N. Abrams Family
Collection, 1974
Photo courtesy The
Solomon R. Guggenheim
Foundation/Art
Resource, NY
Art © 2018 The Andy
Warhol Foundation for
the Visual Arts, Inc./
Licensed by Artists Rights
Society (ARS), New York

18 Ed Ruscha
*The Los Angeles County
Museum on Fire*, 1965–68
Oil on canvas
53 1/2 × 133 1/2 inches
135.9 × 339.1 cm
Hirshhorn Museum
and Sculpture Garden,
Smithsonian Institution,
Washington, DC
Photo by Cathy Carver,
courtesy Hirshhorn
Museum and Sculpture
Garden, Smithsonian
Institution

19 Graciela Carnevale
Tucumán arde, 1968
Gelatin silver print
30 1/4 × 20 1/2 inches
77 × 52 cm
Part of a larger
collaborative artwork by
the Grupo de Artistas de
Vanguardia also called
Tucumán arde
Archivo Tucumán Arde
(Graciela Carnevale)
Courtesy Graciela
Carnevale and espaivisor
– Galería Visor,
Valencia, Spain

20 Artists' Poster
Committee of Art
Workers' Coalition
(Irving Petlin, Jon
Hendricks, Frazer
Dougherty)
Photograph by
Ronald L. Haeberle
*Q. And babies? A. And
babies.*, 1969
Offset lithography
25 1/8 × 38 1/4 inches
63.8 × 97.2 cm
International Center of
Photography, New York.
Gift of the Artists' Poster
Committee with funds
provided by the ICP
Acquisitions Committee,
2002
Photo courtesy
International Center of
Photography

21 Cildo Meireles
*Inserções em circuitos
ideológicos: Projecto
Coca-Cola (Insertions
into Ideological Circuits:
Coca-Cola Project)*, 1970
Coca-Cola bottles and
transferred text
Each: 9 5/8 × 2 3/8 ×
2 3/8 inches | 24.5 × 6 ×
6 cm
Photo by Dominique
Uldry, Bern. Digital
image courtesy Daros
Latinamerica Collection,
Zurich
Art © Cildo Meireles,
courtesy Galerie Lelong

22 Hans Haacke
*Shapolsky et al.
Manhattan Real Estate
Holdings, a Real-Time
Social System, as of
May 1, 1971*, 1971
9 Photostats, 142 gelatin
silver prints, and 142
photocopies
Dimensions variable
Whitney Museum of
American Art, New
York. Purchased
jointly by the Whitney
Museum of American
Art, New York, with
funds from the Director's
Discretionary Fund
and the Painting and
Sculpture Committee,
and the Fundació Museu
d'Art Contemporani de
Barcelona
Art © Hans Haacke/
Artists Rights Society
(ARS), New York/VG
Bild-Kunst, Bonn

23 Philip Guston
San Clemente, 1975
Oil on canvas
68 × 73 1/4 inches
172.7 × 186 cm
Glenstone Museum,
Potomac, Maryland
Art © The Estate of
Philip Guston, courtesy
Hauser & Wirth

24 Cindy Sherman
Untitled Film Still #21,
1978
Gelatin silver print
8 × 10 inches
20.3 × 25.4 cm
Courtesy the artist and
Metro Pictures,
New York

25 Jenny Holzer
Truisms, 1978–87
Photostat
96 × 40 inches
243.9 × 101.6 cm
The Museum of Modern
Art, New York. Gift of
the artist
Digital image © The
Museum of Modern Art/
Licensed by SCALA/Art
Resource, NY
Art © 2018 Jenny Holzer,
member Artist Rights
Society (ARS), New York

26 Robert Mapplethorpe
Man in Polyester Suit,
1980, 1980
Gelatin silver print
20 × 16 inches
50.8 × 40.6 cm
Art © Robert
Mapplethorpe
Foundation, courtesy
Art + Commerce

27 Josef Beuys
*7000 Eichen (7000
Oaks)*, 1982
Print
23 3/4 × 33 1/6 inches
60.3 × 84.2 cm
Tate / National Galleries
of Scotland
Photo © Tate, London,
2018
Art © 2018 Artists Rights
Society (ARS), New
York/VG Bild-Kunst,
Bonn

28 Adrian Piper
*My Calling (Card) # 1
(for Dinner and Cocktail
Parties)*, 1986
Performance utensil:
business card with
printed text on cardboard
2 × 3 1/2 inches
5.1 × 9 cm
Art © Adrian Piper
Research Archive
Foundation, Berlin

29 Barbara Kruger
*Untitled (We Don't Need
Another Hero)*, 1987
Photoscreenprint on
vinyl
108 7/8 × 209 3/16 × 2 1/2
inches | 276.5 × 531.3 ×
6.4 cm
Whitney Museum of
American Art, New
York. Gift from the
Emily Fisher Landau
Collection
Art © Barbara Kruger,
courtesy Mary Boone
Gallery, New York

30 The Silence=Death
Project
SILENCE=DEATH,
1987
Poster, offset lithography
33 1/2 × 22 inches
85.1 × 55.9 cm
Photo courtesy Avram
Finklestein

31 Felix Gonzalez-
Torres
*"Untitled" (Perfect
Lovers)*, 1987–90
Wall clocks
Original clock size,
diameter: 13 1/2 inches
34.3 cm
Edition of 3, 1 AP
Alice and Marvin
Kosmin Collection
Photo by Maris
Hutchinson/EPW
Studio, courtesy Andrea
Rosen Gallery, New
York, and David Zwirner
Art © Felix Gonzalez-
Torres, courtesy the
Felix Gonzalez-Torres
Foundation

32 Gerhard Richter
*Erschossener 1 (Man Shot
Down 1)* from *October 18,
1977*, 1988
Oil on canvas
39 3/8 × 55 1/8 inches
100 × 140 cm
The Museum of Modern
Art, New York. The
Sidney and Harriet
Janis Collection, gift
of Philip Johnson, and
acquired through the
Lillie P. Bliss Bequest
(all by exchange); Enid
A. Haupt Fund; Nina
and Gordon Bunshaft
Bequest Fund; and gift
of Emily Rauh Pulitzer
Photo courtesy Atelier
Richter
© Gerhard Richter 2018
(0123)

33 Guerrilla Girls
*Do women have to be
naked to get into the Met.
Museum?*, 1989
Photo-offset lithograph
10 13/16 × 28 inches
27.5 × 71.1 cm
Courtesy
guerrillagirls.com

34 David Hammons
In the Hood, 1993
Athletic sweatshirt hood
with wire
23 × 10 × 5 inches
58.4 × 25.4 × 12.7 cm
Private collection
Photo courtesy Tilton
Gallery, New York

35 Shirin Neshat
Rebellious Silence, 1994
RC print and ink
46 5/8 × 31 1/8 inches
118.4 × 79.1 cm
Photo by Cynthia
Preston
Art © Shirin Neshat,
courtesy the artist and
Gladstone Gallery,
New York and Brussels

36 Rick Lowe
Aerial view of *Project
Row Houses* during
Round 41, curated by
Ryan N. Dennis, 2014
Photo by Peter Molich,
courtesy Project Row
Houses

37 Kara Walker
*Gone: An Historical
Romance of a Civil War
as It Occurred b'tween
the Dusky Thighs of One
Young Negress and Her
Heart*, 1994
Cut paper on wall
Installation dimensions
variable; approx.
156 × 600 inches
396.2 × 1524 cm
The Museum of Modern
Art, New York. Gift
of The Speyer Family
Foundation in honor of
Marie-Josée Kravis
Digital image © The
Museum of Modern Art/
Licensed by SCALA/Art
Resource, NY
Art © Kara Walker,
courtesy Sikkema
Jenkins & Co.,
New York

38 Chris Ofili
The Holy Virgin Mary,
1996
Acrylic, oil, polyester
resin, paper collage,
glitter, map pins, and
elephant dung on canvas
99 3/4 × 71 3/4 inches
253.4 × 182.2 cm
The Museum of Modern
Art, New York. Gift of
Steven and Alexandra
Cohen
Photo by Johansen
Krause

39 Francis Alÿs
Still from *Re-enactments*,
2000
Two-channel video
installation
5 minutes 20 seconds

40 Banksy
Flower Thrower, 2003
Screenprint
19 5/8 × 27 1/2 inches
50 × 70 cm
Private collection
Photo courtesy Christie's
Images/Bridgeman
Images and Pest Control
Office, Banksy, London,
2004

41 Kerry James Marshall
Black Painting, 2003–6
Acrylic on Plexiglas
72 × 108 inches
182.9 × 274.3 cm
Glenstone Museum,
Potomac, Maryland
Photo courtesy Blanton
Museum of Art, The
University of Texas at
Austin

42 Paul Chan
*Waiting for Godot in
New Orleans*, 2007
Performance view,
Lower Ninth Ward,
New Orleans
Creative Time, New
York, and the Classical
Theatre of Harlem
Photo by Donn Young
Courtesy the artist
and Greene Naftali,
New York

43 Shepard Fairey (after Mannie Garcia)
Barack Obama "HOPE" Portrait, 2008
Hand-finished collage, stencil, and acrylic on heavy paper
69 9/16 × 46 1/4 inches
176.7 × 117.5 cm
National Portrait Gallery, Smithsonian Institution, Washington, DC. Gift of the Heather and Tony Podesta Collection in honor of Mary K. Podesta
Art © Shepard Fairey/ObeyGiant.com

44 Ai Weiwei
Remembering, 2009
9,000 backpacks arranged on the facade of Haus der Kunst, Munich
Dimensions variable
Haus der Kunst, Munich
Photo © Jens Weber, Munich, courtesy Ai Weiwei Studio

45 Tania Bruguera
Tatlin's Whisper #6 (Havana Version), 2009
Decontextualization of an action; stage, podium, microphones, one loudspeaker inside and one outside the building, two people in military outfits, one white dove, one minute of censorship-free speech per speaker, 200 disposable cameras with flash
Dimensions variable
Courtesy the artist

46 Pussy Riot
Christ the Saviour Cathedral Performance, 2012
Photo by Sergey Ponomarev, courtesy AP Photo

47 Thomas Hirschhorn
Preparatory sketch for *Gramsci Monument*, 2013
Photo by Romain Lopez
Courtesy the artist and Dia Art Foundation, New York

48 SUPERFLEX (Jakob Fenger, Rasmus Nielsen, and Bjørnstjerne Christiansen)
Hospital Equipment, 2017
Fine-art print on archival paper mounted on Dibond
48 3/8 × 64 1/8 inches
123 × 163 cm
Photo by Gregor Brändli
Art © SUPERFLEX, courtesy von Bartha

49 Luz (Rénald Luzier)
Charlie Hebdo cover, No. 1178, January 14, 2015
Photo courtesy the artist and *Charlie Hebdo*

50 Theaster Gates
Stony Island Arts Bank, 2015–ongoing
Chicago, Illinois
Photo by Tom Harris
© Hedrich Blessing, courtesy Rebuild Foundation

Social Forms
A Short History of
Political Art

Published by
David Zwirner Books
529 West 20th Street,
2nd Floor
New York, New York
10011
+1 212 727 2070
davidzwirnerbooks.com

Editor
Lucas Zwirner

Project Manager
Mary Huber

Copy Editor
Dorothy Feaver

Proofreader
Michael Ferut

Image Researcher
Elizabeth Koehler

Design
Neil Donnelly

Production Manager
Jules Thomson

Color Separations
VeronaLibri, Verona

Printing
VeronaLibri, Verona

Typefaces
Gill Facia, Eldorado

Paper
Multi Offset, 120 gsm

Publication © 2018
David Zwirner Books

Text © 2018 Christian
Viveros-Faune

All artwork © 2018 the
artist, unless otherwise
noted or with the
additional credits listed
on the previous six pages

Distributed in the United
States and Canada by
ARTBOOK | D.A.P.
75 Broad Street, Suite 630
New York, New York
10004
artbook.com

Distributed outside
the United States and
Canada by
Thames & Hudson, Ltd.
181A High Holborn
London WC1V 7QX
thamesandhudson.com

ISBN 978-1-941701-90-4

Printed in Italy

Library of Congress
Cataloging-in-
Publication Data

Names: Viveros-Fauné,
Christian, author.
Title: Social forms :
a short history of
political art / by
Christian Viveros-
Fauné.
Description: New York :
David Zwirner Books,
[2018]
Identifiers: LCCN
2018033417 | ISBN
9781941701904
(soft cover)
Subjects: LCSH: Art—
Political aspects. | Art,
Modern—Themes,
motives.
Classification: LCC
N72.P6 V58 2018 |
DDC 709.04—dc23
LC record available at
https://lccn.loc.gov/
2018033417